Superior Supervision

Don + Sig Weidenweber —
I look forward to your
publications someday :
Don for poetry and Sig
for East Germany experience.
Best wishes.

— Ray Loen
3-7-94

Superior Supervision
The 10% Solution

Raymond O. Loen

LEXINGTON BOOKS
An Imprint of Macmillan, Inc.
NEW YORK

Maxwell Macmillan Canada
TORONTO

Maxwell Macmillan International
NEW YORK   OXFORD   SINGAPORE   SYDNEY

Library of Congress Cataloging-in-Publication Data

Loen, Raymond O.
 Superior supervision : the 10% solution / Raymond O. Loen.
  p.   cm.
 ISBN 0-02-919091-6
 1. Supervision of employees.   I. Title.
 HF5549. 12.L63 1994
 658.3'02—dc20
                                                          93-40137
                                                             CIP

Lexington Books
An Imprint of Macmillan, Inc.
866 Third Avenue, New York, N.Y. 10022

Maxwell Macmillan Canada, Inc.
1200 Eglinton Avenue East
Suite 200
Don Mills, Ontario M3C 3N1

Macmillan, Inc. is part of the Maxwell Communication
Group of Companies.

Printed in the United States of America
printing number

1 2 3 4 5 6 7 8 9 10

To my wife, Lin,
and our daughter, Pamela,
who inspired me to write this book.

Contents

Foreword

During my college years I had a summer job working in a steel warehouse in Detroit. The work was reasonably strenuous, the pay was good, and I learned a lot about how relationships between people took place in a 'down and dirty' environment. I worked the afternoon shift with a group of guys who had been there forever, and their supervisor, a foreman named Joe, was typical of most such folks.

The most vivid memory I have of Joe is his habit of using the same words over and over, to express anger, surprise, admonishment, or to instill discipline—"*The minute my back is turned...*" It said, more that anything else could, everything you needed to know about his management style. To Joe supervision meant giving orders (not coaching) and checking up (not trusting). There was little room in Joe's world for delegating, planning, motivating, or improving. In fact, motivation was administered in a very loud voice whenever someone "messed up."

Unfortunately, Joe is still with us in many organizations. And he holds the first-line administration of our organizational futures in his hands. It's a fact that the most sensitive job in the coming decades will be that of the supervisor. More change in traditional behavior and attitude is required at these strategic organizational positions than anywhere else. And less has been done to equip these people to make the changes required for their success. Supervisory training is often nonexistent, and our newly appointed supervisors learn their skills through observing other supervisors, and by remembering how their parents and teachers instilled discipline in them.

Ray Loen has examined the principles required for effective supervision very carefully and he has crafted a work that will serve as a handbook for initiating and sustaining change at the supervisory level. He tells what to do and what to avoid in a practical and immediately useful fashion. In fact, Ray Loen talks as much about leadership as he does about supervision, and as much about personal interactions as he does about work.

In a larger context the ideas contained herein set the stage for the revolution that's taking place within our organizations. Fewer layers of management and broader spans of control mean that traditonal supervisory behaviors won't work any longer. If we are to be successful, if our organizations are to truly become more productive, our supervisors will necessarily spend less time supervising employees in the traditional sense and more time leading employees using the skills and the practical advice Ray Loen gives us.

Harvey K. Brolin, President
The American Productivity & Quality Center

Acknowledgments

I am indebted to the many supervisors with whom I have worked and from whom I have learned in my role as a management consultant. All have contributed to the content of this book. Some have contributed indirectly through our mutual efforts to determine how supervisors can be most effective. Others have contributed directly by providing me with materials and examples. Included are: Michelle Avolio, Ed Brumley, Don DeFreese, Howard Fuhrman, Rosanne Hoffman, Don Jones, Drew Lippay, Linda Livermore, Katie Lynch-Pontifex, Russ Martineau, Gary Meddaugh, Richard Meeker, Rick Pay, Dan Potter, and Neil Smith. Molly Dahms provided patient and capable word processing help. Senior Editor Beth Anderson helped me make this book a much better product than I would have without her professional direction and warm style.

Introduction

Superior Supervision provides a new perspective on supervision. It's a perspective that supervisors at all management levels in all kinds of organizations have observed in part but not in full. It's about the relatively few things that supervisors must do to perform in the upper 10 percent of supervisory performance. For *superior* supervisory performance, I call the required skills and behaviors *The 10% Solution.*

When you apply *The 10% Solution* to your supervisory job, you optimize your performance. You get the results you intend. You get the support of those who report to you, your peers, your management, and those who use or are dependent on your products or services. You avoid problems. You avoid worry. You may even avoid suffering. In short, you excel.

Among all supervisors, some perform in the top 10 percent and some perform in the bottom 10 percent. Most perform in the middle 80 percent. This book is not for those who are content to perform in the middle 80 percent. It's for those who want to perform in the top 10 percent and who want to avoid performing in the bottom 10 percent. At the top, they excel; at the bottom, they fail—if not in relation to other supervisors, then at least in relation to the needs of their positions and in relation to their potential as supervisors.

In *Superior Supervision* I cover twelve areas of supervisory responsibility. For each area, I describe the best single way for supervisors to excel—to perform in the top 10 percent. For contrast, I also describe the best single way for supervisors to fail—to perform in the bottom 10 percent. This book will help you to excel more and fail less. Or to put it another way: This book will give you *The 10% Solution* for *Superior Supervision.*

Superior Supervision

1

The 10% Concept

Are you aware that:

What you do to excel—in the upper 10 percent of performance—or to fail—in the bottom 10 percent of performance—can impact your career more than what you do in the middle 80 percent of your performance?

George Johnson is a front-line production supervisor in a medium-size manufacturing company. He had an overtime problem: His employees wanted time off rather than more overtime work. His boss, Pearl Major, told him that she would back him in whatever steps he took to meet the production deadlines—except, she said, "We can't add another shift yet. The economics don't justify it. I suggest you find a way to get your people to accept the overtime."

George gave fleeting thought to the idea of calling his people together and telling them he had no alternative but to insist on continued overtime work divided evenly, as in the past, among all of them. But he realized that might cause resentment even if he got compliance. He knew from past experience that resentment could lead to other problems, such as product defects, absences, employee turnover, and even injuries. So he checked with a couple of his key people and asked what they thought the solution was. They suggested a shift meeting to get input from everyone. George knew he couldn't turn the overtime problem into a committee decision, because he was responsible and it was his job to decide. But he felt employee input would be valuable, so he held the meeting.

George and his people considered whether to try to get re-prieves on customer deadlines; they considered ways to improve methods such as faster equipment setup; and they considered ways to reduce reruns. Finally they decided that overtime was the best alternative, but that it should *not* be divided evenly. They suggested overtime be divided according to individual situations and willingness to work the overtime. For example, an employee who had an important family obligation should be allowed to defer, exchange, or reduce his or her overtime assignment. One employee insisted on no overtime at all due to night school commitments. What all of the employees did want was as much notice as possible—something beyond same-day request to work the overtime.

George accepted the group input and said he would act on it immediately. The only qualification was that he had to clear the new overtime procedure with his boss, as other departments might be affected now or in the future. Pearl Major gave her approval for a trial period. George implemented the new procedure, and it worked well. After several months, management got additional equipment, which reduced the need for overtime.

George excelled in the way he handled the overtime problem. On a scale of one to a hundred, he functioned in the upper 10 percent of supervisory performance. He did so because he tapped bottom-up power, the support he engendered from his people. Also, he developed his solution among those affected, his people.

Not all supervisors excel. In George's situation, many supervisors would have performed satisfactorily, but they would not have excelled. They might have promoted teamwork among employees, or they might have tried to convince individual employees to do their share of the overtime. In all likelihood, these supervisors would have performed in the average range of performance—depending on the amount of cooperation they got from their people to solve the overtime problem.

A few supervisors would have failed by quoting a higher level of authority or by claiming their hands were tied. The likely result would have been employee resentment and poor employee performance. These supervisors would have functioned in the bottom 10 percent of performance.

If you had faced George's overtime problem, would you have excelled? If not, *Superior Supervision* will give you guidelines about how to get cooperation and solve problems. If so, *Superior*

Supervision will give you guidelines about how to excel in other areas of supervisory responsibility.

Superior Supervision covers twelve areas of supervisory responsibility:

Job Description for Supervisors

Job Purpose: *Get planned results through those who report directly to you.*

RESPONSIBILITIES:

Plan: Determine what needs to be done by whom by when at what cost for a planning period such as a month, quarter, or year

Delegate: Assign work, responsibility, and authority so your people can make maximum use of their abilities

Give instructions: Give day-to-day assignments to your people so they will do what you want done when you want it done in the manner you want it done

Get cooperation: Help your people work willingly and effectively as individuals and groups

Solve problems: Develop and implement solutions to day-to-day supervisory problems

Staff: See that a qualified person is selected for each of your positions

Train: Teach individuals and groups how to do their jobs

Motivate: Determine and help your people meet their personal needs for tangible and intangible compensation over both short and long range

Counsel: Hold private discussion with an individual about how he or she might do better work, solve a personal problem, or realize ambition

Improve: Develop better methods and procedures to ensure quality and to increase productivity

Handle pressure: Fulfill responsibility in the face of emotional stress or pressing demands

Control: Measure progress and take corrective action when needed to achieve your objectives

As a supervisor, you have responsibility for those who report directly to you. So, for example, supervision occurs between a president and his or her vice presidents—between vice-presidents and directors—between directors and managers—between managers and supervisors—and between supervisors and workers. Although it has application higher up, the focus of this book is at the first and second levels of responsibility—close to where most of the work gets done in an organization.

In each of the 12 areas of responsibility, you can perform in the upper 10 percent of supervisory performance, the middle 80 percent, or the bottom 10 percent. *Picture it this way:*

SUPERVISORY PERFORMANCE CHART

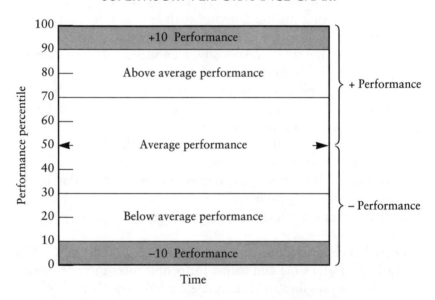

Time

Over a period of time—say, a year,—your supervisory performance ranks anywhere from the bottom to the top compared with that of other supervisors. If your performance ranks in the top 10 percent, you have performed between the ninetieth and one-hundredth percentiles. If your performance ranks in the bottom 10 percent, you have performed between the zero and tenth percentiles.

When you perform at the fiftieth percentile, you are at average performance—the average performance compared with other supervisors. Performance above this is *plus*, and performance below this is *minus*. The range for average performance is plus or minus 20—from the thirtieth to seventieth percentiles. Above-average performance is from 70 to 90; below average performance is from 10 to 30.

To excel, you must perform in the top 10 percent compared with other supervisors—what I call *+10 performance*. When you fail, you perform in the bottom 10 percent compared with other supervisors—what I call *−10 performance*. The idea is for you to perform as much as you can at +10 performance and to avoid −10 performance. This way you excel more and fail less.

Most of us remember best the person who shines and the person who bombs. We tend not to remember good old Joe or reliable Jane who can always be depended upon but whom nobody really notices. That's why what you do to excel or to fail has more impact on your career than what you do between these two extremes in the middle 80 percent of supervisory performance.

I introduced each of the next twelve chapters with the one way I have found that you can have +10 performance and the one way I have found that you can have −10 performance. They follow opposite each area of supervisory responsibility.

Superior Supervision

The 10% Solution: *Excel more by achieving +10 performance and fail less by avoiding –10 performance.*

Responsibility	+10 Performance	−10 Performance
Plan	Create dollar impact.	React to what happens.
Delegate	Let your people out-perform you in their work.	Outperform your people in their work.
Give instructions	Recognize critical instructions	Treat all instructions the same
Get Cooperation	Tap bottom-up power.	Rely on your authority.
Solve Problems	Develop solutions with those affected.	Take unilateral action.
Staff	Extend the curve of past performance	Stress personal chemistry
Train	Accelerate experience	Rely mostly on OJT (on-the-job training)
Motivate	Motivate according to their needs	Motivate according to your needs
Counsel	Act on early-warning signs	Let crises develop

Responsibility	+10 Performance	− 10 Performance
Improve	Commit to improvement goals	Defend the status quo
Handle pressure	Respond rationally	Respond emotionally
Control	Control your own performance	Let others control your performance

As a management consultant, I put a summary of my findings and recommendations at the beginning of each of my reports. So you have here a summary of this entire book. The summary is rather naked now, but it will have much more meaning for you after you have read, and perhaps studied, each chapter.

To give you further indication of what *Superior Supervision* entails, I have a quiz for you. The quiz has one item for each of the twelve areas of supervisory responsibility. You are to check either +10 or − 10 to indicate whether each item represents excellent or unsatisfactory supervisory performance. You will find the correct answers after the quiz and in detail in a subsequent chapter.

Superior Supervision Quiz

	+10	− 10
1. Give equal weight to all of your major responsibilities when you plan.	___	___
2. Ask your people to get your approval whenever they have to spend money.	___	___
3. Let your people deviate from standard procedures whenever they decide it's in your organization's best interests.	___	___
4. Ask your boss to back you in your decisions only when you're right.	___	___
5. Have your people adjust to problems caused by other departments.	___	___
6. Give more weight to sound reference-checking than to personal interviews when you hire a new employee.	___	___
7. Limit your training primarily to what your people can apply on the job.	___	___

	+10	−10
8. Motivate your people primarily by treating them well—good pay, good benefits, good working conditions, and so on.	_____	_____
9. Discuss personal problems with your people only when they come to you.	_____	_____
10. Encourage your people to make only those improvements that are large enough to be reflected directly in accounting reports.	_____	_____
11. Concentrate on helping your people avoid future problems in customer service rather than criticizing them for past mistakes.	_____	_____
12. Make estimates of weekly costs for control purposes if you do not receive your cost report when you need them.	_____	_____

Following are answers to the questions on the quiz:

1. *−10 Performance.* You will be more effective when you plan if you give the most weight to your major problems and opportunities—especially those that have the largest dollar implications. For example, you may need to plan improvements in your safety program if your safety record is poor. On the other hand, you may not need to include safety in your planning if your safety record is excellent; a safety maintenance effort may be adequate.

2. *−10 Performance.* If you require your people to get your approval for each expenditure they make, you become a bottleneck to their performance and you communicate distrust. What you can do is delegate—set up procedures and controls and train your people in them. Then your people can spend money just as effectively as you—especially for routine expenditures such as for parts or repair help.

3. *+10 Performance.* No one has ever developed standard procedures to cover every situation. So instruct your people when and how to use their own judgment to deviate from standard proce-

dures that may not apply in a particular situation—especially when there might be a gain or loss of significant dollars. Recently I called my bank to complain about what I thought was an unfair but legal charge to my account. The bank employee listened, tried to defend the charge, but then gave me a credit when she decided she might be jeopardizing the relationship with a long-standing customer of the bank.

4. *+10 Performance.* Of course you want your boss to back you when you make decisions, but both of you run the risk of getting in trouble if you make the wrong decision. With a wrong decision, you run the risk that your people will rise up in arms against you if they feel seriously threatened. Then the authority of your position as supervisor will mean little or nothing. Your boss should back you only if you're right. Then both of you are likely to get and maintain the cooperation of your people.

5. *−10 Performance.* Your organization needs departments that integrate their efforts and work effectively together. When another department is causing problems for your people, it is your responsibility to develop solutions among those affected—including those in other departments. Otherwise, each department tends to function as an island.

6. *+10 Performance.* During the interview process with a new employee, you get to know your candidate over a period of hours or days. Compare that knowledge with that of your candidate's prior bosses or work associates who have seen your candidate perform over a period of years in all kinds of work situations. With sound reference-checking, you can generally get more valid information about a candidate than you can in interviews where both you and your candidate are likely to be on your best behavior.

7. *+10 Performance.* Unless your people can apply what they learn, why do they need the training? As distinguished from education, which is generally provided by schools, the training you do needs to be tailored to individual jobs. The best way to train is: Train to do. This is a moot point, however, if the only training you offer is on the job—an expensive and time-consuming way to train.

8. *−10 Performance.* Your employees want to be treated well, but there is no limit to the amount of pay or other benefits they will accept and perhaps even seek. What motivates most employ-

ees is the work itself—if jobs are designed well and if supervisors seek to tap the potential of their people. The best single way to motivate your people is to use them well.

9. *–10 Performance.* If your employee's personal problems are affecting his or her work—as evidenced, for example, by tardiness, absences, mistakes, or injuries—then it is your responsibility to act. You must take the initiative to find out what is troubling your employee and to suggest sources of help.

10. *–10 Performance.* Very few improvements will be reflected directly in accounting reports. What will be reflected is a series of continuing improvements—whether they be large or small. An accompanying benefit is your employees' openness to constructive change, which in some instances will be initiated by others inside or outside of your organization.

11. *+10 Performance.* The best way to handle pressure situations such as mistakes by your people is to respond rationally—take positive corrective action to achieve future results. If you respond emotionally through criticism, for example, you are likely to upset your people also. Further, you will communicate greater concern for placing blame than for solving problems.

12. *+10 Performance.* When you do whatever is necessary to get the information you need for control purposes, you are fulfilling your responsibility to control. Otherwise, you are letting others control your performance and you are abrogating your responsibility to control. Not that you shouldn't rely on others. But if they let you down, you need to make your own arrangements to get the information you need, even though it may not be as complete or accurate as you would like.

So much for the quiz. How did you do? Where your answers are the same as mine, you have reinforcement for some of the ideas in this book. Where your answers differ from mine, you have the opportunity to gain new insights in this book.

Note my use of the phrase *your people*. In no way do I mean to suggest that you own those who report to you. However, it's the best generic term I've found to describe those through whom a supervisor is responsible for getting planned results. In your organization, you may use one or more terms, such as *team members, crew members, staff, department, professionals, employees, work-*

ers, direct-reports, or even *subordinates,* a term that is phasing out. It depends on your organization's culture. The terms *co-workers* and *associates* are fine when used in the context of a supervisor's style but not when used in the context of a supervisor's responsibility. The trend toward employee empowerment has caused us to re-examine the language we use, but some confusion has also resulted.

Regardless of the terms you use to describe those who report directly to you, you want to supervise as effectively as you can. This book describes how you can do so through +10 performance in each of twelve areas of supervisory responsibility—the 10 percent solution for *Superior Supervision.*

2

Plan

+10 PERFORMANCE: Create dollar impact

−10 PERFORMANCE: React to what happens

> *Are you aware that:*
>
> You can get most of your results through a few of the things you do?

Kathy Spencer is controller for a distributor of automotive products. She has a staff of eight. The routine of her job—accounting, cash management, budgeting, tax management, banking, and financial reporting—takes up 60 to 70 percent of her time. She knows she must get these activities done, even though management tends to take them for granted. Beyond that, she wants to make a noticeable contribution to her firm. So she now prepares an annual plan covering nonroutine activities for her department. Here is her most recent plan:

Controller's Annual Plan

Planned Activity	Estimated Project Value
1. Install and implement a new computer system designed for distributors	$50,000
2. Supervise accounting staff training on new accounting application programs	50,000
3. Revise general ledger chart of accounts	30,000
4. Improve month-end financial reports	30,000
5. Implement company's new 401(k) profit-sharing plan	20,000
6. Restructure objectives and action plan for new accounting supervisor	20,000

7. Install individualized program to strengthen abilities and increase productivity of key employees in accounting	15,000
8. Revise quarterly incentive plan for accounting people	10,000
9. Develop and begin implementing a loss control and safety program for all company employees	10,000
10. Research potential for self-funded health insurance plan	5,000
11. Conduct company survey to get accounting department performance evaluation by accounting users	5,000
12. Install cross-training and job exchange program among accounting personnel	5,000
Fiscal year objective—total estimated project value	$250,000

Someone once said, "It's just as important to do the right things as it is to do things right." That's what planning is for—to help you do the right things. In Kathy's case, she has identified twelve major actions—beyond the routine of her job—to be accomplished over a twelve-month period. All of them are improvements, with an estimated total project value of $250,000. The estimated value of each project is not necessarily exact; it is based on the judgments of Kathy and her boss. What these estimated values do is give Kathy guidance about where to spend her time. The first four projects have more value than the remaining eight projects, so those are her priorities. Her personal inclination might be to spend her time on other projects or activities, but the estimated dollar values remind her where she can make the largest contributions.

Every organization is dependent on dollars to achieve its potential. That is why supervisors should think dollars. That is why supervisors should develop and implement plans that enhance the dollar value of their efforts to create dollar impact. In her plan, that is what Kathy has done. So relative to her responsibility to plan, she has +10 performance.

Many supervisors do little if any planning. Instead, they react to the challenges and problems that develop or become urgent. As a result, schedules get out of control. Employees don't show up. Quality defects increase. Interdepartmental cooperation deteriorates. Equipment breaks down. Accidents happen. Deliveries are late. Customers complain. Costs get out of line. A crisis atmosphere exists. Supervisors know that preventive planning would help, but they feel victimized, or they're so busy, they feel they don't have time to plan.

Supervisors who function primarily in a reactive way—reacting to what happens—find themselves meeting the same challenges and solving the same problems over and over. They maintain an unsettled rather than a productive working atmosphere. Relative to their responsibility to plan, they have −10 performance.

Other supervisors do only the planning that is required of them. Typically, they help implement the plans of their management and they participate in budget preparation, but they lack plans of their own beyond those of a day, a week, or a couple of weeks in advance.

Still other supervisors feel they have little need to plan. They work in a machine-paced or process-controlled environment such as food or beverage production. Their production is scheduled for them, and their job is to meet the schedule with the people, equipment, materials, and space that have been assigned to them. Each day is a copy of the day before. These supervisors may have to do a little operational planning, but they can get by without doing much planning beyond that. They may not know it, but they are not realizing their potential to plan—especially in making improvements.

The kind of planning I like to see supervisors do is related to what their organizations are trying to accomplish for their fiscal year. Most organizations have to make an annual report to their shareholders, members, constituents, or others. So, to optimize future accomplishment and to have good annual reports, they make annual plans for sales, revenues, profits, distributions, memberships, number of people served, value delivered, or other accomplishment—often in relation to longer-range plans such as for five years. With complementary annual plans, supervisors help make a broader accomplishment for their organization. For changing or unpredictable working environments—as in organizations that are new or do not have a solid financial base—annual planning may be impractical; however, I believe every supervisor can plan for at least a month or a quarter.

Planning for a month or a quarter is short-term, so your only need may be to make a task list—a list of major actions to take. Such actions are a part of annual planning, too, but you have additional considerations for annual planning.

Annual Planning Guidelines

1. List major strengths and weaknesses for your area of responsibility.
2. Draft a one-sentence strategy.
3. Draft an annual dollar objective.
4. Draft major actions.
5. Draft monthly objectives.
6. Do contingency planning.
7. Develop a budget.
8. Finalize the annual plan.
9. Prepare a bar chart.
10. Get approval and implement the plan.

Marv Benson is sales manager for a weekly newspaper, with responsibility for display advertising sales (display sales). He has eleven people, including eight sales representatives. Recently he developed an annual plan covering his firm's fiscal year, starting in April and ending in March. Let's see what he did.

1. *List major strengths and weaknesses for your area of responsibility.* Marv began his planning process by listing four major strengths and four major weaknesses for his assigned area of responsibility, the display sales function. The strengths were: a stable and expanding advertiser base, a large group of prospects for display advertising, an effective marketing program to promote advertising, and a strong sales force. The weaknesses were: a lack of tenured salespeople, burdensome operational procedures, an undeveloped co-op advertising program, and no plan to expand regional and national advertising. When he developed these lists, Marv considered his major problems and opportunities, the potential threats to his effectiveness such as competitive actions, and the major trends affecting his function, such as the economic health of the customers and prospects in his marketing area.

2. *Draft a one-sentence strategy.* A strategy is the major method for accomplishing an objective. With a strategy, you try to exploit your strengths and avoid your weaknesses. Your strategy should be tailored to your current situation, and it should be short so that your people and your boss can understand it easily. Marv developed this strategy: Create new sales of display advertising through target account selling, product-positioning marketing (the amount an advertiser should allot to display advertising in a weekly newspaper out of a total advertising budget), and selling skill development. Note that he developed his strategy before he set his annual dollar objective. He believes in planning without numbers before planning with numbers. Before he set his objective, he wanted to determine whether his strategy would enable him to set a higher objective than he might have otherwise. If he concentrated on helping his salespeople improve certain selling skills, for example, perhaps he could expect to achieve greater results than he had anticipated.

3. *Draft an annual dollar objective.* Many sales managers set objectives for sales volume only. Marv wanted an objective that reflected his concern for profitable sales. So he decided on an objective for dollar contribution, which is sales less those costs that he controls—number of salespeople, sales compensation, promotional expenses, and so on. Earlier he had participated in the corporate planning effort, so he knew the sales that were expected of him to support corporate objectives.

4. *Draft major actions.* Marv developed fourteen major actions to implement his strategy and to achieve or exceed his annual objective. He listed them in order of their dollar impact—those that he felt would contribute the most toward his annual dollar objective—and by giving them primary and secondary priority. He included some actions designed to achieve both current and future results—beyond this fiscal year. For example, he planned to begin implementing a co-op advertising program and to test the market to attract regional and national advertisers.

5. *Draft monthly objectives.* The way to achieve an annual objective is by achieving one piece at a time. So Marv divided his annual objective into twelve monthly targets, with adjustments for seasonal factors.

6. *Do contingency planning.* How do you respond if things go much better or much worse than you originally planned? The purpose of contingency planning is to identify possible contingencies and to develop conditioned responses should those contingencies occur. Marv identified these positive contingencies: Sales exceed plan by 10 percent or more; new special sections of the newspaper are added; and newspaper circulation exceeds target by 10 percent or more. He identified these negative contingencies: Sales fall short by 10 percent or more; unexpected loss of sales personnel; newspaper story or column damages sales effort; and merger of competitors creates major new competitor. Marv wanted a preliminary mind-set (a track to run on) for how to respond to each contingency so he developed conditioned responses. His conditioned responses for the first positive contingency—above-target sales— were: Add sales representative to exploit sales trend; promote newspaper circulation; and implement next year's planned radio campaign. His conditioned responses for the first negative contingency—sales shortfall—were: Analyze target account program, evaluate sales compensation plan, improve staffing, and reduce costs of marketing program.

7. *Develop a budget.* Budgets are for operating expenses and capital expenditures. At planning time, Marv anticipated only operating expenses, which he budgeted as follows:

Sales compensation with benefits	$369,380
Travel and entertainment	3,550
Vehicle expense	19,810
Materials and supplies	13,210
Training	1,500
Marketing program	64,175
Depreciation	2,004
Total budget (controllable expenses)	$473,629

In the past, he had a capital expenditure budget for automobiles when his company owned automobiles and one for computer equipment that is currently adequate.

8. *Finalize the annual plan.* It's only when you see how all of the elements fit together that you can finalize your annual plan. That's the reason several of the planning guidelines begin with the

word *draft*. Marv made a few changes in his numbers and in a couple of planned actions as he finalized his plan.

9. *Prepare a bar chart.* You can use multiple pages to prepare your plan, but I like to see it summarized on one page. This way, your plan is easy to refer to and use. Marv's summary is shown in the bar chart on page 18.

The placement of each bar indicates when Marv will concentrate his time on that planned action. No doubt he will spend time every week on his target account effort, for example, but he plans to concentrate his effort in April, June, August, October, December, and February. The bars also show which actions Marv plans to concentrate on each month. In April, for example, he plans to concentrate on the actions numbered 1, 2, 5, 6, and 7 of primary priority and action number 1 of secondary priority. (Note that the smallest bar is for two weeks—half a month. If an action doesn't require that amount of attention, it probably doesn't belong in your plan as a major action.)

The chart also shows Marv's annual objective, strategy, and monthly targets, including fiscal year-to-date (YTD) targets. Marv's operating budget for controllable expenses is the difference between his sales objective and his objective for dollar contribution. Not shown here are Marv's contingency plans, but he could have included in his bar chart an item for regular follow-up and possible revision of his contingency plans.

Perhaps the biggest advantage of the bar chart is that it shows when each major action is to be accomplished—including when each action is to begin. That's missing in plans that show only deadlines or target dates, and it is a major reason many such plans don't get accomplished.

10. *Get approval and implement the plan.* To implement their plans, supervisors need to get approval from their bosses and support from their people. Marv got the okay from his boss, who asked that he distribute copies of the bar chart to the other supervisors in the event that mutual cooperation was needed. Then he met with his sales staff and explained to them when and how he would be relying on them to help him develop and implement actions for each item in his plan.

I don't know whether you have worked with bar charts, but when you accomplish what each bar represents, you fill in the

FISCAL YEAR PLAN FOR DISPLAY SALES MANAGER

Primary Objective: $1,164,371 dollar contribution (Display sales of $1,638,000 less $473,629 in controllable expenses)

Strategy: Create new sales of display advertising through target account selling, product-positioning marketing, and selling skill development.

Activity	Apr	May	June	July	Aug	Sept	Oct	Nov	Dec	Jan	Feb	Mar
A. Primary priority												
1. Implement program to get $300,000 new sales from target accounts												
2. Develop/implement product-positioning marketing program												
3. Develop/conduct selling skills training program												
4. Staff and train two sales people												
5. Develop/implement sales program related to planned editorial features												
6. Develop/begin implementing co-op advertising program												
7. Get twenty (20) testimonial letters to support sales effort												
8. Test market for regional and national advertisers												
9. Develop/install system for sales operating controls												
10. Update and extend business plan												
B. Secondary priority												
1. Schedule/conduct field sales training												
2. Streamline ad input procedures between sales and production												
3. Streamline credit and cash-with-order procedures for sales people												
4. Establish quality controls for order entry by sales people												
Monthly dollar contribution (000)	74	70	84	91	83	114	113	117	158	70	89	101
YTD dollar contribution (000)	74	144	228	319	402	516	629	746	904	974	1,063	1,164

space above each bar. Suppose that by the end of May, for example, Marv had accomplished everything except item B1 (field sales training). He would fill in all of the bar spaces through May except for item B1. Also, if he had already accomplished half of the June work on item A9 (sales operating controls), he would have filled in half of that item's bar for June to show he was ahead of plan on that item. Marv intends to give his boss a monthly updated copy of his bar chart and to review his progress against the plan.

Marv's total time investment to prepare his annual plan was only a day or two, although he had made notes and thought about it over a period of about a month. The point is that it was not a burdensome process. As a matter of fact, his planning inspired him. In effect, he felt he had his own business within a larger business—with the same concern for dollars as if he owned his own business.

In the event you can't plan for a full year, you can follow the same planning guidelines for a shorter period of time, such as six months. However, I urge you to work toward developing and implementing an annual plan to fit what your organization is trying to accomplish.

I'm sure you've seen this sign:

> PLAN AHEA
> D

It shows the kind of result we get if we don't plan or if we don't plan well. At the same time, a plan will never guarantee results. However, advocates of *Superior Supervision* know that the better they plan, the more likely they are to achieve the results they seek.

3

Delegate

+10 PERFORMANCE: Let your people outperform you in
their work
−10 PERFORMANCE: Outperform your people in their
work

Are you aware that:

The extent to which you outperform your
people in their work can cause you to
work longer and harder than you need to?

Juan Lopez is an entrepreneur in the landscaping business. He
offers design, construction, and maintenance services. He has
anywhere from ten to twenty employees, depending on his workload. He wants to expand his business but he feels completely
dead-ended. Why? He says he can't get and keep good people. De-
scribing their work habits, he says, "They do just enough to get
by. They don't seem to care. I have to check on them all of the
time." He goes on to say that often when he gets employees
trained, they leave. "They don't usually leave for better pay," he
explains. "They give me some phony excuse like they want to cut
down their commute time or they want to take some time off."

Juan's employees have a different perspective. They feel that no
matter how hard they try, it seems that there is nothing they can
do to please Juan. They feel that he holds back on what they need
to know, and then he criticizes them for not doing the work right.
In time, they develop a fatalistic attitude.

Juan knows landscaping extremely well. He has a degree in
landscaping and worked for three prominent firms before he
went off on his own. He has all of the technical competence he
needs, but he is becoming consumed with people problems. He

observes, "This would be a good business if it weren't for the type of people it attracts." Then he goes on to complain about the long hours he has to put in and that he never has time to take a real vacation.

One doesn't have to be a brain surgeon to see what Juan's problem is: poor delegation. He has become a superperformer, a super-doer, but never really trusts his people to perform. He can and does outperform them in *their* work. He is in effect competing with them about how best to do their jobs.

How well do you delegate?

Many supervisors think they're delegating when they assign work. But asking, "Would you please do this?" or "Would you please do that?" is not necessarily delegating. Delegating occurs over a period of time. It occurs only when you assign work, responsibility, and authority so that your people can make maximum use of their abilities.

A firm that has an outstanding reputation for good delegating is Nordstrom, a national specialty retailer. Management has delegated to its salespeople full responsibility for customer service. Not only do salespeople have freedom to determine how they will promote and make sales, they are also empowered to do whatever is necessary to make the customer happy. For example, recently I bought five on-sale shirts at one of its Portland stores. Later, I discovered that I had remembered my sleeve length incorrectly; I have thirty-four-inch rather than thirty-five-inch sleeves. I tried wearing one of the shirts but found the cuffs riding my hands. I took all five shirts back to the salesperson I had dealt with, but he informed me that the shirts were sold out and there were none left to replace mine. Was that the end of it? No. "I'll tell you what we can do," he said. "We'll just shorten all ten sleeves." And that's what they did, at no cost to me. No waiting—no hesitation—no supervisory approval. Maybe that's why I just spent a couple of thousand dollars on clothes there.

When you delegate effectively, here's what you are saying to your people:

> I trust you to perform. I even trust you to incur costs within the bounds of established policies and budgets. My obligation is to make sure you have the capability, the skills, and the freedom to do your job. If you make mistakes, I will accept the responsibility be-

cause we gain more by the many good decisions you make than we lose from the few bad decisions you make. The more responsibility I can give you, the more opportunity I have to seek and accept greater responsibility. The result is greater efficiency and value delivered to those we serve.

When you delegate in this way, you are letting your people outperform you in *their* work. This is the way for you to have +10 performance relative to your responsibility to delegate. There are instances, however, when you need to roll up your sleeves and pitch in. Such an instance might be when you have an unexpected tight deadline that you must meet.

Let's examine further the issue of trust, by which I mean the confidence you have in your people and, to a large degree, the confidence you have in yourself as a supervisor. Please respond to the nine questions that follow.

To What Extent Do You Trust Your People to Perform?

	Often	Rarely
1. Do you give detailed instructions to your experienced people when making assignments?	_____	_____
2. Do you give your experienced people solutions to problems in their areas of responsibility without first getting their recommendations?	_____	_____
3. Do you take over from your experienced people when there is an important task to be done?	_____	_____
4. Do you do the troubleshooting when there is a problem or crisis?	_____	_____
5. Do you require your people to get your approval when they need to spend money or incur costs on routine matters?	_____	_____
6. Do you require your people to go through you when they need help from another department or when they want to see upper level management?	_____	_____

	Often	Rarely

7. Do you expect your people to accomplish results primarily through your methods when there are alternatives?

8. Do you give your people minimal information about costs, prices, margins, sales, production, profits, or planned changes?

9. Do you tend to be intolerant of mistakes your people make?

If you answered "often" to one or more of the items, you have an opportunity to improve your delegating. Let's see why.

1. *Do you give detailed instructions to your experienced people when making assignments?* If so, you may say, "I'd like you to do this, and here's how I'd like you to do it." There are times when you must give your experienced people detailed instructions, but if this is your routine, you are relying more on yourself than on them about how to do their work.

2. *Do you give your experienced people solutions to problems in their areas of responsibility without first getting their recommendations?* A good way for you to outperform your people is to solve their problems for them. Make no mistake: They will seek your solutions if they find that is what you want. If they know you like to feel needed, they will make you feel needed. Just as bad: Some supervisors will solicit recommendations from their people but then they'll respond, "That may be okay, but I wouldn't do it like that."

3. *Do you take over from your experienced people when there is an important task to be done?* Early in my career, I did a lot of field sales training. I'd let the new salesperson make the sales presentation, but then I'd find myself taking over to close the sale. This was appropriate for demonstration purposes, but not at the point when the salesperson needed to practice closing. Even with experienced people, many supervisors take over to make the sale, design the product, select the supplier, or make the commitment for their people. But supervisors are to get results through their people, not for their people.

4. *Do you do the troubleshooting when there is a problem or crisis?* From time to time manufacturers have equipment or process failure with very expensive downtime. When this happens, some supervisors can't resist getting right into the middle of the action to do the *technical* troubleshooting. I'm sympathetic with their intent, but they have only *supervisory* responsibility for troubleshooting. The *doing* responsibility belongs to their people. Supervisors should involve themselves only when their people need help or are not following appropriate procedures. If you are doing troubleshooting that could be delegated, you are neglecting problem-solving opportunities at a higher level of responsibility with larger dollar implications.

5. *Do you require your people to get your approval when they need to spend money or incur costs on routine matters?* If so, you run the risk of being a bottleneck for meeting the routine needs of your people to do their jobs. What you can do is provide them with standard procedures about what costs they can incur plus when and how to do so in what amounts.

6. *Do you require your people to go through you when they need help from another department or when they want to see upper-level management?* Many supervisors are insecure and want total control over everything their people do. If you want to avoid giving that impression, develop standard procedures for interdepartmental contacts—again, to give your people freedom to perform. Your worst fear may be that Mac, Mary, or Marshall will go around you to complain to your boss about you. Trust your boss to handle the situation constructively and, perhaps, to ask your employee to go through you first in the future. Avoid repressive measures if you want a productive atmosphere where delegation can thrive.

7. *Do you expect your people to accomplish results primarily through your methods when there are alternatives?* You may be tempted to insist that your people use your methods to sell, buy, solve, or produce. After all, your methods served you well—perhaps by selling through customer entertainment, or buying with emphasis on price, or producing through long work hours. But suppose your staff members want to sell by relying more on customer service, or they want to buy on the basis of total value received, or they want to produce by working more efficiently. If they

get the results you want, how important is it really that they use your methods? Not very, if you want them to rely on themselves.

8. *Do you give your people minimal information about costs, prices, margins, sales, production, profits, or planned changes?* Maybe you know about the mushroom treatment. This occurs when supervisors keep their people in the dark and feed them a lot of manure. Often supervisors do not share margins or profit information because they fear that their staff members will misuse it and, for example, seek higher pay or incur unnecessary waste. I have found the reverse to be true: Employees respond positively and responsibly when you trust them with dollar information, such as value of production, cost of materials, cost of overtime, margin on orders, prices charged, value of customers, and corporate profit. Without such information, employees tend to perform indifferently or with resentment based on wrong perceptions. They especially resent reticence about important changes that will affect them— such as new methods or equipment to be installed, or plans for expansion or downsizing, or moves to new locations. When you delegate fully, you share information, and you trust your people to use it to do their jobs better and to respond constructively.

9. *Do you tend to be intolerant of mistakes your people make?* If you were brought up in a critical atmosphere or have perfectionistic tendencies, you are likely to be somewhat intolerant of mistakes that your staff makes. This is especially true if you were trained in a profession such as engineering, accounting, law, or medicine. The result may be that your staff sees you as being unduly critical. To avoid criticism, your people will rely more on you than on themselves. In effect, they will insist that you outperform them and your delegation efforts will be torpedoed.

What we've been discussing are really ways in which supervisors have −10 performance relative to their responsibility to delegate. By contrast, you can have +10 performance by following six delegating guidelines, all of which will help you let your people outperform you in their work.

Delegating Guidelines

1. Distinguish supervising from doing.
2. Assign to each of your positions maximum responsibility and authority.

3. Establish a standard procedure whenever your people come to you repeatedly with the same need.
4. Give your people the freedom to make mistakes.
5. Maintain big-picture control.
6. Get periodic input from your people to improve your delegating.

1. *Distinguish supervising from doing.* You can't be a good delegator unless you can distinguish when you are supervising from when you are doing. You are *supervising* when you are trying to get planned results through your people by planning, delegating, instructing, getting cooperation, solving problems, staffing, training, motivating, counseling, improving, handling pressure, and controlling. You are *doing* when you are performing tasks that could be done by an employee—whether or not you actually have an employee to whom you can delegate. Examples of doing are:

- Make a computer requisition for materials
- Close a sale for one of your qualified salespeople
- Take an order from a customer
- Make a routine settlement of a customer claim
- Do a statistical analysis for daily quality control
- Improve the design of a product or process
- Prepare a chart showing financial results
- Do aging of accounts receivable
- Purchase new equipment
- Give a talk to a professional or trade group

You will always do some tasks, because there is no one else to do them or because you are in the best position to do them. But when you have people who are qualified and trained to do them, your job is to delegate and rely on them as much as possible.

2. *Assign to each of your positions maximum responsibility and authority.* Today many supervisors let their staff members order their own materials or supplies, resolve scheduling conflicts, inspect for quality, make rework decisions, get emergency repairs, shut down production lines, do their own estimating, give discounts from list process, decide on customer credits, and so on. These are activities that supervisors used to reserve for themselves because they felt their people couldn't perform them adequately.

That may have been true in an earlier day, but now employees are becoming better educated and better qualified to contribute more to their organizations. The guiding principle is this: Those closest to the work are in the best position to make decisions about the work.

3. *Establish a standard procedure whenever your people come to you repeatedly with the same need.* You are performing best if your day-to-day operation functions as well without you as with you. So if your people can't function well without you, ask yourself why. It may be because they feel they need your help or approval regularly. If that is the case, see if you can establish one or more standard procedures about who will do what when. Chances are your standard procedures can cover 80 or 90 percent of the situations your department will face and that it will perform as well as if you were involved.

4. *Give your people the freedom to make mistakes.* Most of us dislike criticism and try to avoid it. If your people feel they are being criticized to the point that they won't act or make decisions without your approval, you have a delegation problem. Your people will perform best if they feel confident and if they know you will react constructively to any mistakes they make. Together you can decide how to avoid future mistakes.

Tasha Ludlow is a sales manager of metal-fabricated products. She gave one of her sales representatives, Phil, the authority to make certain estimates without getting her final approval. Phil sold a good-size order that unfortunately turned out to have a miscalculation for a major cost item. Rather than blame Phil, however, Tasha took the responsibility for what had happened and developed with Phil a way to validate the accuracy of the cost item on future estimates. She continued to let Phil make estimates without her final approval, and he performed in the field with improved capability and confidence.

5. *Maintain big-picture control.* You are responsible for achieving planned results for output, revenue, customer service, cost control, and the like. You are more likely to achieve such results if you keep your eyes on the forest rather than on the trees. This means that you should avoid nitpicking about how your people do their jobs and avoid distracting your people with what they see as minor concerns. What difference does it make if your people

develop their own methods for noncritical activities or if they deviate from scheduled work breaks but still get their jobs done? On the other hand, you must avoid giving your people so much freedom that you lose control of the achievement of planned results.

6. *Get periodic input from your people to improve your delegating.* Your people are not likely to volunteer suggestions about how you can improve your delegating—how you can rely more on them. So if you want this type of input, you will have to ask them for it—say, once or twice a year. Use a "you" rather than an "I" approach. For example, ask individuals: "What would make your job easier?" or "What bottlenecks might we try to eliminate so you can function more effectively?" or "What decisions do you feel you could make that now require approval from me or someone else?" or "What additional duties and responsibilities might make your job more valuable to our organization?"

Now suppose you agree with all six of these delegating guidelines, but you have a boss who expects you to stay abreast of details you would normally delegate. That can be a nasty challenge, but there are actions you can take. One approach is to sit down with your boss and tell him or her about your delegating dilemma. Then suggest an alternative way for your boss to get the desired information, such as by going directly to your staff or by providing your boss with periodic reports yourself. Another way is for you to get agreement with your boss about your monthly targets. Then you can refer to your accomplishment against these targets if he or she pushes you for details you have delegated. If you persist in this manner, chances are your boss will ease off.

Delegating is so all-encompassing that at times it may seem synonymous with supervising. It isn't; it's only one part of supervising. However, it is the foundation of supervising. When you do it well, you are well on your way toward *Superior Supervision*.

4

Give Instructions

+10 PERFORMANCE: Recognize critical instructions
−10 PERFORMANCE: Treat all instructions the same

Are you aware that:

You can ruin weeks, months, or years of good supervisory performance by giving one poor instruction that results in a large dollar loss to your department or organization?

Carl Carlson is production manager in a medium-size commercial printing company. One day, the company's top salesperson, Karen Kopinsky, came to him with an urgent request. "We have to redo the Krimpax catalog order," she explained, "because we fouled up. We didn't make the proof changes they requested, and they can't send out the catalogs as they are."

Carl knew the importance of handling customer complaints promptly, so he promised a quick response. He checked, and sure enough, Karen was right: Someone had mislaid the proof changes, and they hadn't been made. With that, Carl called Karen. "What do we have to do to satisfy the customer?" he asked. Karen responded, "Redo the catalog. I thought I'd already made that clear." "When does Krimpax need the catalog?" Carl asked. "Right away!" Karen responded. Carl detected irritation in Karen's voice so he didn't pursue the matter any further with her except to say, "Okay, I'll take care of it."

Carl proceeded immediately to his production scheduler. He explained, "We need to slot a redo—the Krimpax catalog. Here are proof changes we need to make. Please give it a priority scheduling."

A week later the sales manager asked Carl to come to his office. "Carl," he said, "we have a problem. You inserted that Krimpax job into our schedule, and it impacted deliveries for three other customers—all of whom are worth many thousands of dollars more per year to us than Krimpax. You took Karen at her word, but I'm confident she could have worked something out with Krimpax to give us some breathing room on their needs. We can't change what happened, but I'm hoping that in the future we can prevent similar occurrences. What do you think?"

Fortunately, Carl resisted his temptation to react defensively. One reason was that he didn't want the sales manager to involve the president—their common superior—after all, this kind of incident could affect the president's attitude toward Carl and color his upcoming performance evaluation. Instead, Carl got the sales manager's ideas about how to handle the next scheduling conflict. They developed measurable criteria and devised procedures to make scheduling changes when there were conflicting demands among priority orders.

Here the outcome was positive. No long-term damage was done. Carl even took his performance from −10 when he gave instructions to +10 when he improved the scheduling procedures. But it is easy to see how Carl's simple instruction to the scheduling person could have had more serious repercussions, especially for Carl himself.

My earliest recollection of what can happen with a bad instruction that has large dollar implications involves an incident when I was a youth back on the farm in South Dakota. We had just completed harvesting the oats. This cleared the field and made it possible for us to let the cattle out into the field to graze and to eat grain spillage. Next to the oats field but not separated by a fence, we also had a field that had a thriving crop of six-foot green corn. My dad told my younger brother, "I'm going to let the cattle out into the oats field, and I want you to watch them." Dutifully, my brother did as he was told.

An hour later, Dad happened to notice that all the cattle were in the adjoining corn field eating up a storm. He almost had a conniption, because cattle can bloat and explode when they overeat an entrée as delectable as green corn. The cattle were a major asset for our parents, and Dad could visualize two dozen cattle lying motionless with their feet up. Excitedly, he ran over to my brother. "Hey, I told you to watch the cattle!" "I did," my brother responded quizzically. "I know where every one of them is." Well, Dad had never read a book or taken a course on how to give instructions. He gave my brother Hail Columbia (an old expression), wherein he made very clear that my brother had jeopardized the well-being of the whole family—seven of us.

This incident nonetheless had a positive outcome. Dad corralled the whole family, and we finally got the cattle out of the corn field in time to prevent disaster—no mean task, as cattle move only one step with each prod when they're in gastronomical heaven.

No doubt you can think of instances where you or a supervisor you know has given instructions that had costly results. In my own supervisory seminars, every group cites examples where supervisors gave instructions that resulted in large dollar losses such as these:

Example 1: $100,000 of metal in solution was pumped into a waste system, due to a wrong instruction about which valves to turn

Example 2: $50,000 of unnecessary software development costs were accrued, because of an instruction to rely on proprietary rather than off-the-shelf software

Example 3: $20,000 in production was lost from equipment breakdown, due to an instruction to run the equipment past the point of critical maintenance and repair

Example 4: A $10,000 order was lost to the competition, because of an instruction to delay settling a complaint on a previous order from that customer

Example 5: $7,000 was lost due to material price increases, because of an instruction to stay within the material purchase budget

Example 6: A $5,000 above-bid cost for fabrication done at the installation site rather than at the factory resulted because the instructions about specifications were not clear

Example 7: $3,000 was expended in unreimbursable overtime, due to an instruction to meet a shipment deadline

Example 8: $1,000 was lost to extra freight costs, due to an oral instruction that caused misdirected shipment

Every day supervisors give thousands of similarly costly instructions. They tend to treat all of their instructions the same and don't distinguish which ones are critical, with significant dollar implications. One result is they have –10 performance in giving instructions. Consequently, they may not get the raise or increased responsibility they expect. They may even get demoted or fired. Management usually remembers those who have cost their organizations unnecessary dollars.

Why do supervisors give costly instructions? The biggest reason is they do not distinguish critical instructions that have significant dollar implications from those that do not. Another reason is that they may be people-oriented, production-oriented, compliance-oriented, or cause-oriented, rather than dollar-oriented.

If you are *people-oriented,* you tend to give priority to what your people think—especially what they think about you. You bend over backward to get and maintain their acceptance. For example, suppose you are a sales manager who wants to make some changes in account assignments. If your people object or offer resistance, you may defer too much to them and not achieve what you intended.

If you are *production-oriented,* you tend to give priority to goals, schedules, equipment, materials, methods, and budgeted costs. You may give inadequate attention to the attitudes of your people when it is obvious to you but perhaps not to them why a certain goal or deadline must be met.

If you are *compliance-oriented,* you tend to give priority to established policies and procedures. You refer your staff members to the manual or the memo or the standard practice or the budget when they face certain problems or challenges in their jobs. If it's not standard practice, you tell them they can't make the adjustment or give the credit or spend the money regardless of the potential economic loss or benefit.

If you are *cause-oriented,* you tend to give priority to the medical, social, political, religious, or other cause that your organization champions. So when you make a nonroutine assignment, you may give more priority to an individual's devotion to the cause than to his or her capability to perform.

How can you have +10 performance relative to your responsibility to give instructions? Most important is that you distinguish which are your critical instructions. A critical instruction is an assignment you give in a nonroutine situation where you can make or lose significant money—say, a thousand dollars or more. It differs from a routine or standing instruction.

Most of your instructions are routine. You have established ways of doing things, and you make repeated assignments to the same people on whom you know you can rely. A standing instruction is a standard policy or procedure that covers such items as work rules, order scheduling, quality requirements, requisitioning, and record-keeping. You're not likely to have problems with routine or standing instructions. However, you may have problems with critical instructions. With such instructions, one mistake can cost your organization significant dollars, and management may see you in a bad light.

You probably don't give a critical instruction very often—perhaps only once a week or so. But when you do, you want to be able to recognize it. You can tell that your instruction might be critical by the situation you're in. Such situations are nonroutine.

Nonroutine Situations Where Your Instructions May Be Critical

1. You are meeting special needs of:

   - Large customers, clients, users, or prospects
   - Vital suppliers
   - Your management
   - Other departments or people on whom you are dependent
   - Financing sources such as banks, investors, or donors
   - Any organization or person with a claim or complaint

2. Your people are trained inadequately or resist doing what you want done.
3. You are introducing change: people, products, services, processes, policies, procedures, or methods.
4. You have new needs for legal compliance: EEOC (Equal Employment Opportunity Commission), EPA (Environmental Protection Agency), OSHA (Occupational Safety and Health Administration), ADA (Americans with Disabilities Act), other.
5. You are risking a potential shut-down, product failure, unsuccessful installation, competitive response, or other negative contingency.

Not only do you give critical instructions, you also get critical instructions—from your management and others with whom you work. You will do a better job of giving critical instructions if you recognize those you get and respond to them accordingly.

Suppose your boss says, "Make sure you comply with EEOC and other legal requirements when you fill the position you have open." You know that you cannot exclude candidates on the basis of race, creed, sex, or age. But unless you have studied or been trained in other provisions of the law, you may not know that you and your employer could be held in violation if you seek information about a candidate's marital status, country of origin, or medical history. To avoid getting into potential trouble, you need to recognize that your boss has given you a critical instruction, listed as item 4 above. Then, for example, you may respond to your boss, "Would you mind reviewing for me the particular legal requirements you are concerned about?" or "Are there some new legal requirements I may not know about?" or "Whom do you suggest I contact for an update on employment law?"

When you get other instructions that you recognize as being critical in nature, make sure you explore their implications. First, confirm your understanding of the instruction. Then ask questions such as: "How important is this in relation to everything else I'm doing?" "What events led up to your asking me to do this?" "What kind of dollars are involved—to make or to lose?"

Let's review the eight dollar-loss examples to see how the supervisors could have realized that they were in non-routine situations when giving what turned out to be critical instructions.

Example 1: It seems obvious that the supervisor was dealing with a new or untrained employee if instructions were needed about which valves to turn.

Example 2: The supervisor was initiating change in the form of software development. Also, there was the risk that internally developed software might not work as well as off-the-shelf software, perhaps adapted to the organization's needs.

Example 3: The supervisor was taking a clear risk of a production loss as a result of delayed maintenance and repair of equipment.

Example 4: The customer had special needs in the form of a complaint on a prior order. The supervisor should have seen a red flag and arranged for prompt settlement of the complaint.

Example 5: The supervisor must have known that material prices were going up because of the instruction to stay within the material purchase budget. The supervisor took a risk that could have been avoided.

Example 6: Either the supervisor had factory personnel who were not completely trained or there was a change in the usual type of order. Otherwise, it should have been clear that the final fabrication was to be done at the factory rather than at the installation site.

Example 7: Trying to meet the special needs of a customer may mean the customer will pay for overtime costs if there is prior approval.

Example 8: The misdirected shipment—a negative contingency—was the result of an oral instruction. The supervisor should have given a written instruction or gotten prompt confirmation about where the shipment was directed.

Hindsight is always clearer than foresight. However, these supervisors might have avoided their mistakes if they had remembered that Murphy's law is always working: Whatever can go wrong will go wrong—often at the worst possible time.

Even if you realize that you're in a nonroutine situation giving a critical instruction, you still may not get the results you want. It depends on how you give your instruction. Guidelines for how to do so follow.

Guidelines for Giving Instructions

1. Make a request.
2. Consider timing.
3. Set a deadline.
4. Get feedback.
5. Put certain instructions in writing.
6. Follow up.

1. *Make a request.* When you are busy or in a hurry, you are more likely to give an order or a directive rather than make a re-

quest. Your people are likely to do what you want, but they will listen better and respond more favorably to a request than to an order. That's because by making a request, you imply that they are also busy and are doing work as important as or more important than what you are asking them to do. By making a request, you give them the opportunity to respond and to ask any questions they may have, such as the reasons for your instruction. Also, you come across as communicating to them on their level rather than as their boss from a level above them.

2. *Consider timing.* When you decide to give an instruction, you probably want to give it promptly so you can get on to something else. But what if your employee is preoccupied or upset or has a conflicting commitment or was just going to go on break? Your employee may appear to be giving you his or her attention but may not really be doing so. You may succeed in communicating in this situation if your instruction is short, but if your instruction is long or complicated, you'd do well to ask first whether your employee has a minute or is interruptible.

3. *Set a deadline.* "Can you do this when you get a chance?" "I'd like this as soon as possible." "Can you get back to me right away?" "Please put this on your agenda." If you were the employee, could you be sure of when you were expected to respond to such requests? Surprisingly, I find that supervisors don't always make clear by what date, day, or time they want their instructions carried out. If an instruction is important enough to give, it's important enough to set a mutually understood completion time for it.

4. *Get feedback.* This is probably your most important guideline whenever you are giving a critical instruction. It's the way you ensure that you and your employee have mutual understanding about what you want done. But you must do more than simply ask if you've made yourself clear or if your employee understands.

I recall a plant manager, a former military man, who held meetings with his department heads. He'd ask them to do something; they'd agree to do it; and then often they would not do what he had requested. This drove him crazy. With his military background, this plant manager assumed that when his department heads said yes, they meant yes. What happened was that he had overloaded his department heads—often with conflicting priorities—and when they said yes, they meant, "Yes, we hear you.

We'll do the best we can in relation to everything else you've asked us to do." Further, they were reluctant to give their boss any resistance, as he tended to take it as insubordination.

One reason it's important to get feedback is that words have so many different meanings.

What Do These Instructions Mean?

Fix it.
Take care of it.
Do what you have to do to get results.
Meet the schedule.
Make it a top priority.
Follow our procedures—no exceptions.
Stick to the plan.
Don't go over budget.
Change it.
See me before you decide.

I doubt whether you give simplistic instructions such as these, but if you do, you need to make yourself clear—especially for critical instructions with significant dollar implications. Probably the best way to get feedback is to ask your employee to repeat his or her understanding of your instruction when you feel there's any possibility for misunderstanding. At a minimum, ask whether your employee has any questions. Also observe your employee's body language—facial expression, receptivity to what you're saying, and apparent willingness to do your bidding.

5. *Put certain instructions in writing.* You are taking an undue risk if you do not give written instructions for specifications, dates, dollars, new policies and procedures, and any other matter where you want to hold your people strictly accountable. It's particularly important for you to put in writing any instructions affecting several or all of your people. Too much gets lost with oral transmission. If there's any possibility for misunderstanding of a critical instruction, get one or more qualified people review what you have written. You want to make sure it says what you mean it to say. The written word is naked. It can't begin to reflect what you can say in person, and it can't smile or answer questions.

6. *Follow up*. Busy supervisors tend to assume their instructions will be carried out. If no particular harm can be done if they are not, that's probably all right. But if an instruction is critical, you must follow up to see that the results you wanted were achieved. One way is to ask your employee to report promptly to you in person or by phone when he or she has done what you requested. Another way is to make a follow-up note in your daily calendar at the time you gave your instruction, then follow up your follow-up.

All supervisors give effective instructions in *most* situations. But not all supervisors give effective instructions in *all* situations. It's giving a critical instruction in a nonroutine situation where you can distinguish yourself. It's also where you enhance your reputation for having *Superior Supervision*.

5

Get Cooperation

+10 PERFORMANCE: Tap bottom-up power
−10 PERFORMANCE: Rely on your own authority

Are you aware that:

The power of those through whom you are
trying to get results is greater than all the
power and authority you and your superiors have?

In my supervisory seminars, I present one case that always gen-
erates heated discussion.

> Suppose Joe reports to you, and one day you fire him. Soon there-
> after, it develops you were wrong—either in the reason you fired
> him or the way you did it. Should your boss back you in the action
> you took, or should your boss not back you and, if necessary, force
> you to rehire Joe?

Many supervisors argue that if your boss doesn't back you, he
or she is cutting you down in the eyes of your people, who will
then begin to question how much authority you actually have.
Other supervisors argue that the damage has already been done
and, while it may have been wrong, you should learn from the experience. Further, if you and perhaps some of your people didn't
like Joe, the firing was probably justified in the interests of good
working relationships in any case.

At this point I ask, "Suppose Joe were a member of the union.
Wouldn't you have to rehire Joe?"

"Well, in that case, I guess we'd have to," they usually respond.
Then I postulate: "Are you telling me you'd rehire Joe—do the
right thing—only if you had a union? Don't all employees have the
right to be treated fairly and protected from unjustified dismissal?"

We ultimately conclude that a supervisor's need to always be right, even when he or she is wrong, doesn't hold a candle to the need to treat employees fairly—especially when the decision, such as a firing, can have career-long implications for the employee.

A supervisor's boss should back the supervisor only if the supervisor is right. Although the supervisor may feel undermined by having to rehire Joe, he or she can actually achieve more credibility and authority by correcting the wrong. The supervisor can go to his or her department and say: "As you all probably know, yesterday I fired Joe. I regret to say I was wrong. My boss reviewed the situation with me, and I'm going to ask Joe to come back. I want you to know I'll do my best to avoid making this kind of mistake in the future. As for Joe, please make it easy for him to return."

What does the supervisor say to Joe? How about this: "Joe, I'm calling to apologize and to ask you to come back to work. I found out I was wrong, and I'll do my best not to let anything like this happen again. I've met with your co-workers and given them a similar explanation. They are expecting your return. You can come back tomorrow if that's okay with you."

If you had been the supervisor who fired Joe and took subsequent corrective action, what could we say about your performance?

First, we could say that you functioned at a –10 performance level when you fired Joe. It appears you acted precipitously and in an autocratic or top-down authority mode. Today, no supervisor should have the authority to single-handedly fire anyone—not even where there is gross insubordination. Your authority should be limited to having the employee leave the premises and to *recommending* termination. This is to make sure your action is fair to all concerned and to keep you on safe legal ground. Most likely you would want to get prior approval from your human resources or personnel department, if you have one. Otherwise, you or your boss might want to get outside legal counsel to validate your intended action. If Joe had accosted you, for example, it might develop that he behaved irrationally due to a reaction he had to a medically prescribed drug.

Second, you functioned at the +10 performance level if you took the corrective actions described that tap bottom-up power. In doing so, you sought the support of your people, who could have taken group action had they felt threatened because of what you did to Joe. It's even possible that your people—maybe even Joe—would now think more highly of you than before because of the way you handled the situation. Not every supervisor is objective enough or secure enough to admit a mistake—especially to those he or she supervises. You could have taken the corrective action without admitting you were wrong; in that case your supervisory performance would have been average or above average, but it wouldn't have been at the +10 level. Perhaps you follow the credo: Never apologize and never explain. This is a poor credo for supervisors who are dependent on their employees.

What is bottom-up power, and what are its implications for you?

If you believe that the ultimate power or authority in your organization originates at the top, this belief will be reflected in your supervisory style and in the way you seek to get cooperation. You are likely to be autocratic because you feel you are exercising power and authority that emanates from your superiors. I find this behavior particularly among supervisors who have had to work their way up to supervisory responsibility, who are grateful to management for the positions they have, and who feel insecure about other career alternatives. Of course, you and your superiors have power and authority—but your people do also. You are more dependent on them than they are on you. A supervisor at any level is likely to be replaced if he or she does not get and maintain employee support. If you understand how much power and authority your employees actually have, you will be more democratic in your style and give priority to what they think and feel.

Mistakes that are made at the top of an organization can impact you and your people significantly. I'm thinking of a president who made a top-down decision to change medical benefits in order to reduce costs. The action was a competitive necessity, and the president assumed that that would be clear to everyone. Wrong. The employees got up in arms about what the company was doing to them. Several threatened to quit. Only after considerable backpedaling by the president and other members of management did the employees settle down. Eventually the issue was resolved with the aid of an outside benefits consultant, who was able to present objective data about competitive benefits along with alternative solutions.

How much power and authority do your people really have? Individually, they may not have very much, but as a group, they have a tremendous amount. They can take positive actions to support you, or they can take negative actions to impede you. Here are some examples of each.

Positive and Negative Actions Your People Can Take as Indications of the Power and Authority They Have

Positive Actions	Negative Actions
1. Work productively	1. Slow output
2. Achieve quality	2. Make errors
3. Save time	3. Waste time
4. Maintain attendance	4. Become absent
5. Report facts	5. Generate rumors
6. Support management	6. Bad-mouth management
7. Discuss problems	7. File grievances
8. Keep working	8. Stop work
9. Trust management	9. Unionize
10. Stay with employer	10. Resign

Compare these two columns. With the positive actions that you encourage your people to take, you will excel (+10 performance). With negative actions by your people, you will fail (–10 performance). If your people take more negative actions than positive actions, your position may be in jeopardy, regardless of where you are in the management hierarchy.

Suppose you have one subordinate. You and your subordinate disagree over what each of you feels is a critical issue—say, ethical behavior, safety, or new technology. You both put your jobs on the line over this issue, so strongly do you feel about it. Who is likely to survive, assuming upper-level management must decide in favor of one or the other of you?

Since you have only one subordinate, you are likely to be the one to survive because management will probably feel you are more valuable to your organization.

Now let's assume you have five subordinates. The situation is the same, except all five of them are locked in against you. Who will survive?

Here again, you may be the one to survive over all five subordinates. Your management may see your value as greater than that of the entire group of five.

Now let's assume you have ten subordinates, or one hundred, or a thousand, or ten thousand. Who will survive—you or they? At some point, your management will decide that your value is not as great as theirs, and you will be terminated. It makes no difference whether you're objectively right or wrong about the critical issue. It's the *perception* that your people have that counts because, as a group, they have the power. What *they* think is more important than what *you* think. The reason they have the power is that there are more of them than there are of you. And in most instances, management will see the value of a group as greater than the value of any one person: you. In other words, the power—and the ultimate authority in an organization—is in the numbers. And the numbers are at the bottom of the organizational hierarchy, where the organization's products or services are provided. Like it or not, *might is right,* and it's at the bottom. If you genuinely understand this, it will show in your supervisory style when you try to get cooperation from your people.

A word about unions. No doubt you've heard the expression: Management forms unions. What this means is that employees form or maintain membership in unions because they feel management has not taken care of their needs, such as for pay, benefits, job security, working conditions, and work rules. Employees exercise their bottom-up power to meet their needs because they do not trust—or have not trusted—management to do so. The result is that unions have had to force management to do what it should have done in the first place—give employees fair and equitable treatment.

If you are in a union environment, you can have a mutually productive working relationship. If you are not in a union environment, chances are you'd prefer to avoid one, as it would reflect on the relationships that you and other members of management have with employees. In either case, treat your people as if they were ultimately in control—because they are.

Can you be less than perfect and still be effective? Yes. Your people will take a certain amount of abuse—for example, where you make mistakes or where they disagree with you. Over time, however, they will relate to you on the basis of your overall performance. They are likely to take group action only when many irritations build up or when a critical issue develops, such as discriminatory treatment.

What about your personality? You know you can't change the basic you. And if you are getting the cooperation you want and the results you seek, you have no need to change. That's the catch—*if* you are getting the cooperation you want and the results you seek. If you're not, then you need to change some of your behavior.

Let's look at some of the reasons supervisors don't get cooperation, or at least as much cooperation as they'd like.

Four Reasons Supervisors Don't Get Cooperation

- They have different work assumptions.
- They tend to be insensitive to the concerns of their staff.
- They overlook people's need for self-esteem.
- They are self-centered.

• *They have different work assumptions.* There are five work assumptions that appear perfectly reasonable and that most supervisors probably have: "If I pay you, I expect you to do the work"; "If we begin work at eight o'clock, I expect you to be here"; "If you do the work, I expect you to do it right"; "If the customer needs it, I expect you to get it out on time"; "Your job is to help us meet our profit objectives." However, in my consulting, I've learned that employees do not always share these views. Examples of employee views I've encountered that contradict these assumptions are: "I'd be willing to do the work if others didn't goof off so much"; "I worked late last night and see no pressing reason to be on time this morning"; "I don't get credit when I do it right, so maybe it's not all that important"; "There's only so much a person can do to meet every deadline for every customer"; "Why should I bust my butt to help meet profit objectives? I never get paid more than a competitive rate." These five work assumptions also appear perfectly reasonable. When employees are not cooperating, the supervisor will do better by taking a bottom-up rather than a top-down approach. Most employees will open up if they're asked and if they feel their input will be handled constructively. Perhaps different work assumptions is the problem.

• *They tend to be insensitive to the concerns of their staff.* Many supervisors treat their people like tools of production—as if their people were inanimate. Yet employees have many concerns, to which they often feel their supervisors are oblivious. Examples of employee concerns are:

> Nature of work assignments—desirability, skills required, location
> Participation in policies, procedures, schedules, and other matters that affect them
> Behavior of supervisor toward them in daily contacts
> Equal enforcement of work rules, such as attendance, safety rules, and dress code
> Fairness of pay
> Personal relationships with other employees
> Job security, as indicated by the demand for services
> Equal treatment by supervisor regardless of race, sex, age, sexual orientation, religion, politics, or memberships
> Timeliness of supervisory decisions
> Changes such as in methods, equipment, or relationships
> Progress in responsibility, pay, promotion
> Effect of work on personal matters such as health, family, private interests, and affiliations

Without sensitivity to such employee concerns, supervisors can impede their own effectiveness when they make work assignments, ask for extra effort, or try to make improvements. Supervisors should also keep in mind that employee concerns differ with individuals and change over time.

• *They overlook people's need for self-esteem.* I have over my desk two quotes from Lord Chesterfield:

> People hate those who make them feel their own inferiority.
> Those whom you can make like *themselves* better will, I promise you, like *you* very well.

As a supervisor, you're in a position of authority. You may be more knowledgeable, you're supposed to have broader perspective, and you may have more to do than you can get done. If you're not careful, you may project: "Do it because I say so!" or "It's obvious why we have to do this" or "I just want your agreement, not a lot of flak." Inadvertently, you may make your people feel somewhat inferior. Most people don't want to feel inferior. They want to feel important—that they're trying, that their opinions count. They will cooperate if they understand. In short, they have the same need for self-esteem that you do.

• *They are self-centered.* "If I promote or transfer Nancy, I'll have to hire and train someone else," a supervisor may think. Or: "If we make this change and it doesn't work, I may get a bad performance review." "If we adopt this new idea, Ed may get the credit." "If we assume the responsibility, I'll have more work to do." "If we admit to the error, I'll get hell." These are the kinds of self-centered interests, spoken and unspoken, that some supervisors have. So they say no or they procrastinate or they point the finger at someone else rather than do what has to be done.

Ultimately, psychologists tell us, we make decisions for personal reasons. However, if we're self-centered and don't think through the consequences, we may make decisions at the expense of our people. Then we project: "My interests are more important than your interests." That's not the way to get and maintain cooperation.

Supervisors who don't get cooperation for one or more of the above four reasons give the impression of relying on their authority to get cooperation. Consequently, at times they get –10 performance.

How can supervisors avoid –10 performance and achieve +10 performance when they need to get cooperation?

I doubt whether you have any difficulty in the routine of your job. You wouldn't have been promoted to a supervisory role if you didn't know the basics of working with people. However, there are some guidelines that may help you get cooperation from your people and tap bottom-up power when you have the need for it.

Guidelines for Getting Cooperation

1. Get in-depth knowledge of your people.
2. Identify areas of rapport and difference.
3. Build mutual trust through regular personal contact.
4. Maintain an atmosphere of openness.
5. Solve cooperation problems promptly.
6. Rely on opinion leaders to get group cooperation.

1. *Get in-depth knowledge of your people.* You already know your people, but how *well* do you know them? How much do you know about each employee's knowledge, skills, experience, education, health, family, significant others, friends, cultural background, interests, hobbies, values, affiliations, ambitions, attitudes, and concerns? Maybe even birthdays and anniversaries? Whether or not these subjects are of interest to you, they tell you about a resource on whom you are fully dependent. The more you know about that resource, the more options you have for tapping that resource—particularly when you have a challenging issue such as a reassignment, a cutback, or automation. Your people are more likely to respond favorably if they feel you understand them and have a genuine interest in their welfare.

Probably the best way to get and maintain information about your people is informally over time—weeks, months, years. Be prepared to share with them whatever they want to know about you, too. In a hiring situation, however, avoid seeking any information that is not job-related. In that situation, your good intentions to learn about an employee's age, health, affiliations, and values may be interpreted as unwelcome prying and may be illegal.

Some supervisors know more about their equipment than they know about their people—specifications, capacity, needs for maintenance and repair, cost, useful life. That's where their immediate interests lie. To act like they're genuinely interested in the details of their people's lives might come across as a charade. But even they can develop their interest in people gradually. That's one dimension of personal growth.

2. *Identify areas of rapport and difference.* You are most comfortable when you are with people who are most like you. That's true for your people as well. So if you identify common interests,

hobbies, values, experiences, affiliations, and so on, you will have much more rapport with them than you would otherwise. As for differences in race, religion, upbringing, sexual orientation, and interests, your employees are likely to open up to you if they feel you are genuinely interested in them. You can create a bridge of understanding even if you have no common perspective at all about certain subjects.

3. *Build mutual trust through regular personal contact.* Some of your staff members trust you from the moment you first get to know each other. Others will take a long while to give and receive trust. If you can talk personally with each person every week or two, you are more likely to keep abreast of what they're thinking and feeling. When they see that you use the information about them constructively, their trust in you will grow and you will be able to rely on it when you need it.

Don't be surprised if your people test you and try to shock you with some of their ideas on social behavior, discrimination, environment, politics, and the like. Your best response will be non-judgmental unless the subject is job-related—then it may be appropriate for you to help resolve an issue such as how they can improve their relations with other workers.

4. *Maintain an atmosphere of openness.* If you keep your cards close to your vest, your people will do the same. If you lay out your cards on the table, chances are your people will too. That's the way to treat information. Share with your people information that affects them. Otherwise, rumors will replace facts. Your department can handle bad news like a potential layoff much better than no news. If there's a void of information, your people will observe what's going on around them and create their own answers to questions they have. Further, if they feel you haven't been open with them, they may slow up output to extend their jobs or take other action. Openness carries responsibility, though. There's no need to share information that doesn't affect people yet, such as exploratory mergers or acquisitions. If they ask, you can say that you're always considering ways to help your organization realize its potential and that you'll let them know promptly when and if any decisions are made. If you have to err, however, do so on the side of openness. Then your group is more likely to reciprocate and not catch you by surprise.

5. *Solve cooperation problems promptly.* Problems have a way of growing. So if you can nip them in the bud, you will prevent having to solve bigger problems later on. Attendance is a good example.

Sue Rodman has been an office supervisor for about a year. Recently she hired two employees who had had little work experience. They had good attendance for a couple of months; then one of them began to come to work late. Sue decided not to say anything about the first couple of offenses. After all, she figured, they're adults. Then the other employee began to emulate the first. Sue decided she had better take action, so she sat both employees down and reminded them about their responsibility to be on time. There were no further problems for a couple of weeks. Then the tardiness pattern began to repeat. Sue had already spoken to the offenders so she thought the problem would correct itself. Then the tardiness turned into absences. Sue's other employees began to complain about favored treatment of the new employees. Now Sue had an office morale problem.

Sue got some guidance from her boss and had to terminate one of the new employees. It turned out that each of the new employees was tardy and absent for different reasons. The one who was fired had a social life that interfered with her attendance. The other tended to be somewhat lazy and irresponsible until she found her job in jeopardy. If Sue had taken prompt action with the first tardiness and continued to do so with each subsequent offense, she could have prevented the later eruption of the bigger morale problem.

Most problems relating to employee cooperation start out small. To address them, all you may have to do is talk to your employee—to show that you care and that you're there to help. Take disciplinary action only if you have to. But be willing to do so decisively and promptly in deference to the feelings and attitudes of your other employees.

6. *Rely on opinion leaders to get group cooperation.* Every group has members who are opinion leaders by virtue of their capability, character, tenure, or personality. Therefore, use opinion leaders as a resource, especially to achieve a challenging objective involving some or all of your people.

Wendell O'Neill is field supervisor for a construction company. One day the superintendent asked Wendell, "What can you do to improve our safety performance? Our insurance rates will go through the roof if we don't reduce our lost-time accidents." Wendell responded, "We're doing our best to implement our safety program, but our craftspeople tend to take safety shortcuts when they feel the safety precautions are more trouble than they're worth. Setting up handrails and fall protection, for example, get short shrift at times." The superintendent expressed sympathy, but this didn't prevent him from asking Wendell to move safety from a secondary to a primary priority.

Wendell's fleeting impulse was to go tell his people, "The boss wants us to put safety ahead of output." But he thought better of this course of action and began to think about how he'd go about getting the cooperation he needed.

"Just bugging my people to follow safety procedures would be telling them something they already know," he reasoned. "Threatening them with disciplinary action is an alternative too, but that would wear thin after a week or two."

Wendell concluded he needed long-term support from his employees and that input from them might help. So he decided to talk individually to three opinion leaders among his people. What he found was this:

The regular safety meetings had become routine and lacked meaning.

Employees who followed safety procedures resented those who didn't.

There were no clear rewards or penalties relating to safety.

Individual employees might be willing to assume safety responsibility for their work areas on a rotating basis.

Some injured employees could do work other than their regular jobs.

Wendell thanked his respondents and went to his office to reflect on their input. Then he drafted an employee memo with these safety program revisions:

The objective will be zero lost-time accidents for the remainder of the construction job, and a prominent display will be maintained to show the number of days without lost-time accidents.

An employee in each work area will have safety responsibility for the whole work area on a monthly rotating basis.

Employees will be asked to suggest subjects for regular safety meetings.

Every attempt will be made to reassign any injured but able-to-work employee to temporary work until able to return to regular job.

There will be quarterly awards plus an annual award of prizes to all employees if they, as a group, have no lost-time accidents.

To make sure he had backing from his management—including a budget for the prizes—Wendell reviewed the memo with his superintendent and then with a sampling of four or five employees who were opinion leaders. All responded favorably and advised Wendell to present the safety program revisions to his employees in person. "Use a memo to confirm intended action about an important subject—never to announce it" was the essence of what they reminded him.

After implementation of the safety program revisions, Wendell followed up weekly and then monthly to see that he still had employee support. The last I knew, he and his people had gone a record 243 days without a single lost-time accident. His opinion leaders had proved to be a valuable resource to help him get group cooperation. They were also the means by which he tapped bottom-up power.

Are there times when it is neither practical nor desirable to tap bottom-up power before you take action? Of course. When there's a pressing need to serve a major customer or when there's an urgent deadline, you may not have the time. However, your employees are likely to support you on these occasions if your day-to-day style indicates that you give priority to their interests and that you know they have ultimate power and authority.

I hope you already tap bottom-up power along the lines I've described. If so, what I've done is to document what you're already doing. If this is not your modus operandi, then I urge you to adapt your style accordingly. Then you will strengthen the scaffolding for your *Superior Supervision.*

6

Solve Problems

+10 PERFORMANCE: Develop solutions with those
affected
–10 PERFORMANCE: Take unilateral action

Are you aware that:

You can know the right solution to a day-
to-day supervisory problem but your solution will fail unless you get willing acceptance of those affected?

A sales manager installed a sales contest to increase fourth-
quarter sales, but the salespeople didn't respond favorably to
the catalog prizes.

A shift supervisor installed a housekeeping program, but shift
employees resisted it because they felt they were doing cleanup
that should have been done by the prior shift.

An office manager established centralized office services to handle peak workloads better, but users preferred to continue relying
on their own assistants.

A mill warehouse supervisor took disciplinary action against a
repeat offender of the attendance policy, but he had to rescind the
action because there had not been consistent application of discipline throughout the mill.

A marketing services supervisor developed an audiovisual presentation, but the salespeople used it sporadically or only in part.

A president eliminated company cars for officers in favor of
monthly automobile allowances, but the officers' reaction was one
of grudging acceptance.

These are all examples of perfectly sound solutions to day-to-
day supervisory problems, but they share one common problem of

their own: The solutions did not get the willing acceptance of those affected. The reason was that each of the six supervisors had identified a problem, decided on a solution, and only then told those affected what to do. That is, they took unilateral action. The result was that they had −10 performance relative to their responsibility to solve problems. To have had +10 performance, they would have had to develop solutions along with those who would be affected by them.

Supervisors at all experience levels have difficulties solving day-to-day supervisory problems, in addition to taking unilateral action.

Problems Supervisors Have in Solving Day-to-Day Supervisory Problems

- They let their problems accumulate.
- They don't face up to interdepartmental problems.
- They solve the wrong problems.
- They reinvent the wheel.
- They assume their solutions are working.

- *They let their problems accumulate.* Every supervisor faces a myriad of day-to-day supervisory problems: violations of minor safety rules, tardiness, unauthorized absences, early quits from work, incomplete paperwork, phone abuse, unkempt appearance, break and lunch extensions, and so on. The accumulation of day-to-day problems is itself a problem. Taken singly, few of them seem serious enough to require priority action. Taken together, they can have a noticeable negative effect on a supervisor's performance.

- *They don't face up to interdepartmental problems.* Many supervisors feel it would be presumptuous of them to interfere with the operations of a supervisor in another department. Yet individual departments must work together to accomplish synergistic results for their organizations—indeed, that is their purpose. Every department is dependent on other departments for products or services. Supervisors who do not support their staff in getting full cooperation from those departments on which they depend are letting their people down. Also, they are not serving their organizations as well as they should.

- *They solve the wrong problems.* One office supervisor stated his main day-to-day problem this way: We need better coordination among users of our high-speed copying machine. Implied in this statement is that better coordination among users is the solution. However, a better solution may be to train users in how to avoid copying problems and delays, or to hire a full-time operator, or to set up a system of copying priorities, or to get additional equipment, or to use outside copying services, or to adopt a combination of such solutions. So it is likely the supervisor addressed the wrong problem in his implication that poor coordination among users was the problem. Why did he state his problem this way? He did what many supervisors do: They state problems subjectively—in terms of their own experience or judgment. They include in their description or statement of a problem what they believe are the causes or solutions. When they do this, however, they limit their perspective about alternative solutions.
- Supervisors can state problems either subjectively or objectively.

Two Ways to State Problems

Subjectively	Objectively
1. Our employees need to work harder.	1. We're not getting planned output.
2. Our sales people need an incentive to sell more.	2. We're not meeting sales projections.
3. Our quality standards are too loose.	3. Our product returns are above budget.
4. Our equipment produces too many rejects.	4. We're not meeting our yield objectives.
5. Our PC software is not user-friendly.	5. Our personal computers are not meeting planned use.
6. We need budgets to control costs.	6. Our costs are too high.

When supervisors state problems subjectively, they run the risk of solving the wrong problems. When they state problems objectively—without implied causes or solutions—they open themselves and their people to a variety of solutions.

• *They reinvent the wheel.* Most supervisory problems have already occurred many times in the past, and previous supervisors have developed good solutions to the problems. What works and doesn't work has a history. Yet supervisors often approach their day-to-day supervisory problems as if the problems had never arisen or been solved before. So they make the same mistakes and take the same wrong turns as their predecessors did before arriving at good solutions. Most organizations have a wealth of experience about how to solve the problems currently faced by their supervisors. Also, supervisors in similar or nearby organizations—even competitors—would be willing to share what they've learned if asked. Supervisors who don't know this or don't act to tap such resources do a lot of unnecessary problem solving. A prior solution may not be completely applicable, but it may be adaptable.

• *They assume their solutions are working.* Supervisors who see their workers every day are in the best position to see whether their solutions to day-to-day problems are working. But some supervisors in organizations such as banks, retailers, distributors, and other multilocation organizations have dispersed employees. These supervisors are tempted to assume that once they've solved a problem—such as inadequate compliance with customer service policies and procedures—it stays solved. But this is not always the case. Conditions change and solutions deteriorate. Even supervisors who do see their workers every day may not observe infractions such as phone abuse or tardiness or poor safety practices that they thought they had curbed. Supervisors who take unilateral action are most likely to assume their solution is working because they tend to function independently, ignoring the reactions of those affected.

How can supervisors solve their day-to-day supervisory problems? I recommend a set of six guidelines.

Guidelines for Solving Day-to-Day Problems

1. Select a problem.
2. Validate the problem.
3. Develop a solution.
4. Sell the solution.
5. Implement the solution.
6. Confirm the solution.

1. *Select a problem.* Supervisors always have problems. They have major problems that they should address in their annual plans. They have minor or day-to-day problems that can usually be solved in a day, a week, or a month. In the course of a year, supervisors have many more minor problems than major problems. So the question becomes: How do you know which problems to solve? The answer is:

If you hurt, you act.

Generally, one or two of your problems bug you the most. They are the ones you feel most strongly about and would like to solve. It might be poor housekeeping or dirty company vehicles. So select one problem, and solve it. Select another one, and solve it. And so on. Resolve the minor concerns that you and your people have, and you eliminate the unrelenting irritants that can build up into bigger problems such as deteriorating employee morale.

2. *Validate the problem.* Here's where you ask yourself who's affected by the problem. A supervisory problem affects not only your staff but often people in other departments—Harry in accounting, or Ursula in shipping, or Stan in reception, or Nettie in human resources. Chances are your boss is affected, or at least you may need his or her approval for your solution, such as to begin enforcing a neglected disciplinary policy. Ask some of those affected for their view about the problem. If you find little support for your concern, you'll probably do well to forget it for now. If you find support, get substantiating facts and opinions about the problem—for example, how housekeeping affects customer attitudes about product quality. If you can put a dollar value on what the problem is costing your organization in a year, do so. Information about the estimated dollar value, say, of lost customers, will get the ear of your management, should you need to spend money on housekeeping equipment or services.

3. *Develop a solution.* Start with an objective statement of your problem. Don't say: "My people are careless in maintaining housekeeping standards." Say: "Our housekeeping standards are not being met." Then you can address whether the standards are unclear, or your people feel overloaded, or people from other departments are contributing to your housekeeping problem, and so

on. Next, get suggested solutions from those affected. Even if you find their ideas unusable, at least they know you considered their ideas. Then develop what you feel is the best solution. It may be a combination of various alternatives.

Sometimes supervisors develop half-baked solutions to their problems, which their bosses veto. One boss told me, "My supervisors complain that I procrastinate in approving what they want to do. But I find their solutions are superficial and not thought through. Often their solutions affect the budgets of other departments." In my consulting work as a professional problem-solver, I find checklists to be an excellent method for analyzing and developing complete solutions to problems. On my checklists I use eight M's and an F: men and women, machines, materials, markets, methods, money, management, maintenance, and facilities. I ask myself questions: Which *men and women* are affected by the problem throughout the entire organization? Is there adequate equipment *(machines)?* Are the right *materials* available when they are needed, at proper quality? How are customers or users of the service affected in the *market?* How effective are present *methods* and systems? What are the direct and indirect costs *(money)?* To what extent is *management* doing its job? How much preventive *maintenance* is there? Are the *facilities* in balance with needs?

For more complete problem analysis and solution, I use the list of forty-two P's.

42 Parameters for Analyzing and Solving Problems

Packaging	Presentation
Parameters	Presumptions
Participation	Pricing
Patents	Priorities
Payments	Proformas
Penalties	Probabilities
People	Problems
Perceptions	Procedures
Performance	Procurement
Permanence	Product
Permits	Production
Persuasion	Productivity
Philosophy	Profit

Pilot	Programs
Planning	Projections
Policies	Promotion
Politics	Promptness
Position	Proof
Potential	Proposals
Practicality	Prospects
Precedence	Proximity

Starting with the first item, *packaging* suggests to me that I need to consider how I package my solution—orally, in written form, using charts or photographs, or other. *Parameters* suggests to me that I need to define the boundaries of my problem, such as my need to involve other departments. *Participation* reminds me to let people help develop the solutions that affect them. Farther down the list, *pilot* suggests maybe I should test my solution for a couple of weeks or with only one group before making it permanent or fully implemented. *Problems* triggers my realization that something could go wrong and I'd better make provision for that possibility—perhaps by taking a more active role in the implementation. *Proximity* causes me to think about how to get continuing cooperation from those who are affected and spread out geographically. You may wish to get the participation of everyone affected when you consider the Ps. The better you think through your solution, the better your chances are for getting both acceptance and approval.

4. *Sell the solution.* This is the guideline generally overlooked by supervisors who take unilateral action. Often they expect compliance simply by virtue of their authoritative position. Or they may feel that they aren't salespeople, after all, and shouldn't be expected to have to coddle their staff or others affected. Actually, you go a long way toward selling your solution when you validate your problem and get early participation from those who are affected by it. By letting others help you fine-tune your solution, you make them part of the solution rather than part of your problem. They enable you to make any necessary modifications in your solution, or in the way you communicate it, or in its implementation and follow-up. For example, they may suggest ways you can tailor the presentation of your solution. Your staff people may want to avoid being spotlighted for causing a problem. Your purchasing

people may be interested in making a streamlined purchase. Your salespeople may want a minimum of paperwork. Your accounting people may want timely reports. And so on.

There is one other selling consideration: timing. If you need your boss's approval to spend money, for example, you may want to assess his or her attitude before you present your proposal just then. "How's the boss feeling today?" may be a wise inquiry. Just like other human beings, bosses have moods too. Sometimes they get bad news from their management or have problems away from the job. If your timing is wrong, you may not get approval for what you know is a sound spending proposal. People tend to say yes when they feel good. They tend to say no when they feel bad. Make sure your boss and colleagues aren't preoccupied with other concerns that they feel are more important when you approach them about solving a problem that's important to you.

5. *Implement the solution.* If you've followed the problem-solving guidelines to this point, implementation of your solution should be relatively smooth. As a supervisor, remember to rely on your staff as much as you can. In dealing with other departments, you will probably have to take the lead with other supervisors on whom you will rely for help in implementation. Make sure you have the backing of your boss so that he or she can respond knowledgeably and responsibly to any concerns that come from above or from other organizational units.

6. *Confirm the solution.* Here is where you follow up to confirm that your solution is working. After implementation of your solution, get immediate reactions from those affected. Then check again after two or three days and then weekly for a month or so. You may have to correct misunderstandings or adapt your solution to new faces or conditions in different locations. Once you are confident it is working and will continue to work, your solution may become part of the daily routine. At this point, consider addressing another day-to-day problem in the manner that helped you solve this problem.

Let's see how the problem-solving guidelines work on the job.

Bob Weingarten headed engineering for a prominent pulp and paper mill when it was undergoing a large expansion. He faced a day-to-day problem with interruptions by those who wanted engineering help and his people found it difficult to get their work done. It seemed that everyone in the mill was a user of engineering services and wanted prompt service. In addition, there were outside users such as contractors, suppliers, and inspectors. Bob could have pointed the finger of blame at his users for waiting until the last minute to make requests. Instead, he saw his users as customers and took it upon himself to try to meet their needs while still meeting a pressing schedule of planned output from his department.

First, he stated his problem objectively: "There are excessive interruptions in the engineering department." Second, he listed all those affected—his people, his management, and his users. Third, he met with some of his staff and held a brainstorming session with a representative group of three engineers and three users. His boss suggested he contact corporate engineering for any solutions that had worked elsewhere.

Next, he reviewed his input and developed a solution based on a combination of ideas. The internal actions he planned were:

Make rotating assignments to one engineer who will handle all external requests.

Have a secretary screen requests when the engineer is on special project and should not be interrupted.

Revise the filing system so the drawings are more accessible.

The external actions he planned were:

Meet with frequent users to define guidelines for making requests, including maximum deadline for service.

Have users put the request in writing when the engineering department is likely to have to spend more than fifteen minutes filling it. Such requests need separate scheduling.

Train qualified users in how to use engineering filing systems.

A longer-term action that he planned was to explore the feasibility of setting up a library for central reference service. To sell these planned actions, he telephoned four major users and asked if they'd like to participate in a two-week test period for improving his service to them. He got favorable reactions, so he held the test, which resulted in a clear improvement in service. Then he used the test results to sell the other users on his solution for serving them better. His follow-up consisted mostly of seeing that new users understood when and how they were to make requests.

If you didn't have day-to-day problems, there would be less need for your supervisory position. I'm not suggesting you want to create problems, but I *am* suggesting that you should view them positively. They are an expected and integral part of your job. Seize opportunities to solve them promptly and effectively so you can enhance your contributions resulting from *Superior Supervision.*

7

Staff

+10 PERFORMANCE: Extend the curve of past
performance
−10 PERFORMANCE: Stress personal chemistry

Are you aware that:

The extent to which you like or dislike a
candidate for a job can cause you to make
major staffing errors?

One of my clients is president of a small manufacturing firm.
One day her accountant/office manager resigned. Her firm
had been growing, so she saw this as an opportunity to upgrade
the present position and hire a controller. In particular, she needed
someone who was computer-literate and could overhaul existing
hardware and software systems. Also, she wanted someone who
was a certified public accountant and who could engender the
bank's confidence for the firm's line of credit.

To find such a person, she decided to place an ad in the newspaper. The ad was productive, and she got a raft of candidates. The
one who impressed her most was a man who came across as
manna from heaven—he looked the part, said all the right things,
and could start immediately.

The president knew she should check his work references, so
she asked him for them. The candidate provided only one because
he said he had worked for only one boss over the last ten years.
During the next couple of days, the president tried two or three
times to call the reference, but the reference was never available
and never called back. Then the candidate came by again to
reaffirm his interest in the job. This impressed the president, so
she decided to hire the man with the proviso that his reference
check would be favorable. The new controller started the next

day, and the president followed up on the reference check, who, she learned, was going to be away for a month.

The president never did talk to the reference, and the new controller tackled his job with enthusiasm. The controller established a new chart of accounts, began working on new computer systems, established contacts with the bank, and even proposed new ideas for financing. The president lacked the background to know everything that was happening in the computer area, but she began to get a little nervous when system installation target dates were missed. She got more nervous when she learned that the controller was taking disks home to store back-up copies of data. She really got nervous when she got reports from outsiders about some unbelievable tales the controller was telling about the company. In due course, the president came to this conclusion: She had hired a controller who was a pathological liar.

Fortunately, the president took prompt corrective action. She confronted the controller with some irrefutable facts, the controller resigned, and no serious repercussions resulted for the company. Subsequently, the president hired another controller. This time she took a more disciplined approach to hiring and relied much less on whether she liked or disliked each candidate. She discounted personal chemistry and relied on each candidate's validated past performance as the best single indicator of future performance. The new controller has had excellent performance. The president's staffing performance went from −10 to +10, which can be critical because selecting and retaining good staff is one of the most important responsibilities for supervisors at all levels.

Suppose you have a job to fill. Would you tend to prefer a candidate who is:

Male or female?
Tall or short?
Fat or thin?
Older than you or younger than you?
Dressed conservatively or dressed stylishly?
Groomed conservatively or groomed stylishly?
Light-skinned or dark-skinned?
Extroverted or introverted?
Better educated than you or less educated than you?
More capable than you or less capable than you?

If you are like most supervisors who have answered these questions, you have a preference in each set of alternatives. The point is this: Every supervisor has a certain amount of bias and even prejudice. It's inherent in every human being. If you acknowledge that you have certain biases or prejudices that are emotional, you can make a rational decision not to let a bias or prejudice prevent you from making the best staffing decisions—which is also the way to comply with antidiscrimination laws. If you do not acknowledge that you have biases and prejudices, you are likely to act on them unknowingly. Consider this question: Is the ideal person for you to hire or promote under you someone who is similar to you in:

Physical attributes	Personality
Dress	Intelligence
Grooming	Education
Age	Experience
Sex	Accomplishment
Race	Values
Nationality	Interests
Religious beliefs	Hobbies
Political convictions	Habits
Memberships	Physical well-being
Friendships	Marital status
Geographical upbringing	Sexual orientation
Residential location	Ambition
Native language	

In a word, do you prefer someone with the right chemistry?

Answering this question reveals the spoken or unspoken tendency of every supervisor who has staffing responsibility. Even if you say you lack bias or prejudice, you prefer someone who has some similar attributes. The more similar the individual is to you, the greater rapport you feel. The less similar the individual is to you, the less rapport you feel; yet this individual may do a far better job for you than the one with whom you feel a rapport. In fact, the individual you personally like may bomb—or worse, just get by. Then you simply leave him or her in the position, and you never realize the potential of the position.

Sometimes it even pays for supervisors to staff with people who are clearly different from them because these people bring new perspectives and experiences into the workplace. For example, a big-picture macrofocus supervisor might be aided by a nitpicky micropicture detail-oriented employee. A white male supervisor whose people sell to or buy from women or Hispanics might do well to staff with some women and Hispanics.

At times, you can be successful in staffing when you rely on the chemistry between you and the candidates. Then you feel reinforced about your selection procedure. But it's only a question of time before you will make a major staffing error with attendant impact on your supervisory performance—maybe even on your career when, for example, the position you are filling affects the survival or viability of your organization.

There is no one who does much staffing who has a perfect track record. Staffing methods are not infallible. However, the supervisors who have the worst hiring problems commit certain staffing errors.

Why Supervisors Make Major Staffing Errors

- They rely mostly on personal chemistry.
- They do shortcut staffing.
- They neglect performance reviews during probationary periods.
- They keep looking for the best available candidate.
- They select nonthreatening employees.
- They seek experience or education more than capability.

Let's discuss each of these staffing errors.

• *They rely mostly on personal chemistry.* We've already discussed certain aspects of personal chemistry, but there are more.

Supervisors do consider performance, but often they make staffing decisions based more on whether they like or dislike an individual. Supervisors who have a sense of humor seek the company of those who enjoy humor or who make them laugh. Supervisors who love sports prefer interchange with those who talk teams, players, scores, and rankings or who participate in the same sports they do. Supervisors who are committed to a social, political, or religious cause lean toward those who support their cause. Supervisors who don't like confrontation tend to dislike those who disagree, complain, or challenge. Supervisors who came up the hard way tend to dislike those who have much better formal educations and are progressing faster than they did. Supervisors who are perfectionists tend to dislike those who don't dot all the *i*'s and cross all the *t*'s. Supervisors who make staffing decisions based on such likes and dislikes usually engender resentment. Often the better talent—those with alternatives—leave for jobs with other employers.

I've seen too many staffings where the personal chemistry between boss and subordinate went from sweet to sour when performance faltered. On the other hand, I've seen personal chemistry go from sour to sweet when performance rose above expectations. Sometimes supervisors and chameleons seem to have a lot in common. Am I saying personal chemistry is not a factor in staffing? Not at all—I am saying personal chemistry should not be the *main* criterion for a staffing decision. But it might make the difference where, for example, two candidates appear equally qualified in meeting your main staffing criteria.

For new employees, personal chemistry exerts itself in the interview process. There's a tendency for all of us to feel we are good judges of people: "My gut feel tells me to hire Frank." "My intuition favors Greta." The problem is that during a job interview the candidate is on his or her best behavior, and often the supervisor is trying to sell the candidate on the job. Many a not-so-good candidate has created a favorable impression just by listening. On the other hand, a very good candidate who tends to be shy may come across as shifty-eyed.

One of the worst hiring practices is to make hiring decisions based primarily on the results of daisy-chain interviewing. This occurs when candidates are interviewed by several people who later meet and vote on whom to hire. How much can a group of strangers discern about a candidate in only an hour or two? Yet hiring supervisors repeatedly follow their hunches and give short shrift to comprehensive personal reference checks, more often than not. Everyone has a track record, a curve of past performance that can be validated—even candidates fresh out of school.

Personal chemistry also comes into play when supervisors promote, demote, transfer, or terminate employees.

• *They do shortcut staffing.* Most supervisors have more to do than they can get done. So when they staff, they look for short-cuts. They check the files, place an ad, or call the employment agency—whatever takes the least time and trouble. Even when they have the help of a human resource or personnel department, they tend to separate themselves from the selection process and accept whomever they get. If they have a policy of promotion from within, they select an internal person, whether or not that person is adequately qualified. When they see a resume, they over-rely on it. Resumes are useful but are not always accurate. Sad to say, some candidates misstate their education, their experience, and their accomplishments. Shortcut staffing reminds me of the old refrain: "When I'm not near the one I love, I love the one I'm near."

Employment agencies and executive recruiters do it profession-ally, so you can rely on them—right? No, not often enough. I find that many of them will send you candidates to interview. Then when you respond favorably ("Her resume is on target, and I think she'll fit in."), they promote hiring. Some employment agen-cies and executive recruiters never check references. They may save you time, but they don't always do a good job.

• *They neglect performance reviews during probationary peri-ods.* Many organizations, especially those that are unionized, usu-ally have probationary periods of thirty days or more before new employees can become permanent employees. Supervisors are sup-posed to monitor the performance of each new employee and to do one or more performance reviews. In theory, this works. In practice, organizations often end up with an employee who should have been let go. Reason: The supervisor got tied up with other matters and gave very little attention to the performance reviews.

• *They keep looking for the best available candidate.* "We have to compare several candidates to get the best one" is a common attitude among supervisors. This attitude exists when supervisors don't have measurable criteria for the person they want, so they never know when they've found the best candidate. If the best candidate happens to be the first or second one interviewed, chances are he or she has taken another position by the time all of the candidates get processed.

• *They select nonthreatening employees.* Most of us have some insecurities that can help to motivate us if we channel them constructively. Supervisors usually channel their insecurities destructively when they function defensively. In staffing, they function defensively when they try to protect their own positions by selecting people less capable than themselves. They fear they might be replaced by a bright, hardworking newcomer, so they hire people who won't threaten their own jobs.

Have you heard about the Law of Diminishing Competence? A psychologist came up with this term to describe what can happen in an organization. Let's say the president selects vice-presidents less capable than he. In turn, the vice-presidents select directors less capable than they. The directors select managers less capable than they. Finally, the front-line supervisors select individual performers less capable than they. The cumulative impact on the organization's performance could be disastrous.

• *They seek experience or education more than capability.* An organization with a tight budget usually doesn't want to make much of a training investment, so it seeks candidates with experience. The more experience they have, the better. Unfortunately, candidates with the *most* experience don't always have the *best* experience. I'm thinking of a supervisor who recently hired a lead operator of plastic injection molding machines. The supervisor was in dire need of someone with experience and was delighted to get someone who had done similar work for fifteen years. The supervisor later learned that there was a reason why the employee had been doing the same thing for fifteen years: That was the limit of the employee's capability. What the supervisor had wanted was someone who could train other employees and had supervisory potential.

Supervisors typically want someone not only with experience in their kind of work, but with more formal education than is needed—for example, a college degree, when a high school diploma is adequate. You can measure years of experience or schooling more easily than you can evaluate capability. Yet capability can be far more important than education or prior experience.

There are lots of staffing errors you can make, but you can also prevent them. The best single way to staff well is to extend the curve of past performance. The most reliable indicator of what a candidate will do in the future is what he or she has done in the past. So if you determine what a candidate has done in relation to your needs, you can be fairly confident that the candidate will perform similarly for you. This doesn't necessarily mean that the best candidate is one who has held a similar position. A candidate who performed well in school, for example, may be best qualified to learn new technology in your organization. However, a candidate who has been successful in opening new accounts and meeting sales objectives for a prior employer is likely to do so for you. A candidate who has met challenging production deadlines and has done quality work for a prior employer is likely to do so for you. Such candidates probably have both experience and capability. In these cases, you can place less reliance on candidates who say they can or will perform but lack track records in having done so.

A candidate's track record doesn't have to be limited to specific experience if you are looking for adaptability, creativity, dependability, industriousness, or other talents. You may want to grow you own—mold a capable employee who is inexperienced in your particular business but is able and willing to learn the way you want to do business.

To determine a candidate's past performance and prevent staffing errors, I recommend following six time-tested guidelines.

Staffing Guidelines

1. Develop written qualifications for the candidate you seek.

   - Make the qualifications measurable.
   - Distinguish between essential and desirable qualifications.
   - Identify the kind of past performance you want from the candidate.

2. Recruit one or more candidates.
3. Screen each candidate on the basis of your written qualifications.
4. Hold preliminary interviews to select one or more final candidates.
5. Conduct reference checks to validate each final candidate's past performance.

6. Decide on the final candidate, hold and arrange necessary interviews, and fill the position.

Explanations for each guideline follow.

1. *Develop written qualifications for the candidate you seek.* When you put candidate qualifications in writing, you think through what you want, and you have a communications tool for making your requirements clear to others. Some supervisors use a job description for this purpose, but that describes the job, not the person. What you need are defined qualifications for experience, skills, track record, education, motivation, career potential, and the like. Make each qualification measurable so you can tell with a yes or a no whether a candidate meets the qualification. Instead of specifying that you want a candidate with budgeting skills, for example, specify that the candidate must have at least two years of experience in corporate budget development and administration that can be validated by reference checks or by examples of the candidate's work. Distinguish between essential and desirable qualifications, so you can consider hiring the first candidate who meets your essentials and so you won't have to keep looking for the best available candidate. Make clear the kind of past performance you want—ideally a track record that you can describe with numbers. You must, of course, make sure your qualifications are legal—especially to comply with antidiscrimination laws.

What do written qualifications look like? In the following example, the sales manager for a medium-size manufacturer of food and beverage processing systems recently developed written qualifications to help him find a sales engineer for the eastern market.

Qualifications for Sales Engineer

Qualification	Essential	Desirable
1. Sales experience	Two years of sanitary processing equipment sales at unit prices of $25,000 or more	Over two years selling tanks, pumps, piping, meters, filters, and controls to food and beverage mfrs. in eastern USA
2. Estimating experience	One year developing prices for equipment	More than one year with direct use of

Qualification	Essential	Desirable
	with no preestab-lished list prices	personal computer for estimates of $50,000 to $250,000
3. Persuasive skills	Has track record of selling additional products to present accounts, opening new accounts, intro-ducing new products, and resolving customer problems	Has taken courses or seminars to develop skills in persuading individuals and groups
4. Communications skills	Has used phone and written word regu-larly to do prospect-ing, make appoint-ments, and close sales	Has done written pro-posals showing finan-cial justifications—re-turn on investment, cost analysis, and payback periods
5. Planning skills	Has relied on self mostly to analyze territory, identify key accounts, and manage time based on dollar value of activities	Has had training and done extensive reading on sales planning and time management, in-cluding use of 80/20 rule
6. Track record	Has had account responsibility for annual sales of at least $1 million from existing and new customers	Has opened new cus-tomer sales of at least $1 million within a 12-month period
7. Education	Two years of college or equivalent	BS in engineering or business, plus subse-quent self-development activities
8. Self-motivation	Must be willing to function indepen-dently with long-distance help and direction	Has functioned effec-tively for at least two years with little day-to-day supervision
9. Potential	Mutually profitable relationship within six months	General manager of eastern mfg./sales opera-tion within two years

Do you need written qualifications for internal candidates? You don't if you're promoting a trained replacement from among your people or if you know well the qualifications of someone being transferred to you. Otherwise, it's a good idea. It's one way to avoid getting cast-offs from other departments.

2. *Recruit one or more candidates.* Note that you may need only one candidate if he or she meets all of your essential qualifications. Look first for internal candidates. Then look outside: Get suggestions from present employees, from your suppliers of products and services, and from industry organizations. You can use ads, especially if you need a number of people, but I prefer personal recommendations. Often the best candidates are presently employed and aren't looking for a job. Use the services of your human resource or personnel department, but do not abrogate your own responsibility for staffing. For key or hard-to-fill positions, consider using a recruiting firm.

3. *Screen each candidate on the basis of your written qualifications.* You can do screening by mail, phone, or in person or have someone do it for you. For key positions in sales or management, I like to have promising candidates respond in writing to each qualification. I send them a copy of the written qualifications and ask them to respond about how well they feel they qualify, including what they feel are their most important relevant accomplishments. The idea is to get as much objectivity into the screening as you can. Make sure all the candidates know the compensation level for the job. Proceed further only with those candidates who meet all of your essential qualifications.

4. *Hold preliminary interviews to select one or more final candidates.* Here your purpose is to exchange enough information about your opportunity and each candidate's qualifications so that you can select one or more final candidates. You can do so by phone or in person. Mostly, I find, candidates stress their responsibilities rather than their performance in meeting their responsibilities. Focus your questions on what the candidate has actually done.

5. *Conduct reference checks to validate each final candidate's past performance.* Although both are essential, I give a two-to-one weight to sound reference checking over personal interviews. I do so for both internal and external candidates. There's no way an in-

terviewer can learn as much about a candidate as prior bosses and work associates have learned over a long period of time.

Check by phone or in person at least three work references provided by candidate. References by mail can document factual data, but you will get little, if any, evaluative data. When doing reference checking:

- Validate factual data such as positions held, employment dates, attendance record, safety record, compensation level, and education. Some studies show that as many as one in ten candidates make misstatements about factual matters. Confirm information shown in the candidate's resume or letter.
- Ask for an overall performance evaluation—for example, on a scale of excellent, good, fair, or poor—plus opinions about the candidate's strengths and weaknesses. Include questions about how the candidate responded to pressure, such as tight deadlines, conflicts, criticism, and change. Find out what the references feel were the candidate's main accomplishments.
- Use the written qualifications you developed as a checklist for other information you seek, such as evidence of the candidate's learning ability, adaptability, creativity, dependability, and industriousness.
- Ask why the candidate left or is available and if the reference would rehire the candidate.

While most human resource personnel departments won't supply detailed information, most references will furnish this kind of information if you promise confidentiality and constructive use of their input. You can allude to reference results, but do not disclose them to the candidate.

An example of the information you can get in a phone reference check follows.

Phone Reference Results for Sales Engineer Candidate

I have known him five or six years. I was his boss for two years and have had many subsequent contacts with him.

His performance was excellent in certain areas: people skills, ability to open doors. He got people interested, handled paperwork well, was well organized, kept good customer records, and did good sales reports. In addition, we found him to be conscientious and trustworthy—a person of integrity. His technical knowledge wasn't great; hence, he needed help for the close on large orders of several million dollars. A minor weakness is that he talks a lot and could talk himself into minor trouble.

He had good family support for the travel he did and no chemical dependency problems.

When he was under pressure, he reacted quite normally, such as when he might lose an order. He took over a vacant sales territory. Nobody buys from a stranger, but he built the territory up to $3–4 million in about three years.

His total compensation was as you stated. On small orders up to $1 million, he got a larger commission percentage. On larger orders, he got a smaller commission percentage due to the help the company had to provide.

He left our firm because we had a reduction in force and his job was eliminated. He was offered a job out west, but he didn't want to move. He was not let go.

Yes, I'd rehire him for a sales position. I believe he has sales management potential and maybe even general management potential. However, I wouldn't make a production manager out of him.

6. *Decide on the final candidate, hold and arrange the necessary interviews, and fill the position.* If you have followed the previous staffing guidelines, chances are you already have enough information to select the final candidate. Now it is economical for you to devote whatever time it takes to fill your position. Hold an extensive personal interview with the candidate to:

- Answer any questions the candidate may have;
- Give the candidate a tour of your facilities;
- Review the job requirements;
- Describe the opportunity in relation to the candidate's ambition—pay, responsibility, personal growth, other; and
- Explain the remaining steps in the staffing procedure.

Then arrange interviews where the candidate can meet with your boss and other potential work associates. Get their feedback, and if there are no significant hurdles, meet with the candidate to make the offer and fill your position. Avoid using the mail or fax to make an offer. Do this in person, so that you can resolve any unforeseen problems more readily. Then you can confirm your arrangements in writing.

There's a tendency among supervisors at all levels in all kinds of organizations to give much more time and attention to a capital expenditure than to staffing. Yet over a five-to-ten-year period they may invest as much in an individual as they do in a piece of equipment with a five-to-ten-year life. If you know this and staff accordingly, you have the cornerstone for *Superior Supervision*. The better your people, the better they make you look. And if you aspire to greater responsibility, the more likely your people are to push you up.

8

Train

+10 PERFORMANCE: Accelerate experience
−10 PERFORMANCE: Rely mostly on OJT (on-the-job
    training)

Are you aware that:

Your overreliance on OJT can torpedo the
morale and effectiveness of those you are
trying to train?

Martha Merritt is customer service supervisor for a paper
supply house that serves printers. She and her staff of customer service representatives had been doing a good job until her
company expanded its market. Then she began getting a gradual
buildup of customer complaints such as incomplete orders, wrong
products, late deliveries, deficient quality, and indifferent service.
She observed that complaints were most numerous in those locations where she had hired and trained new people. She decided to
investigate. What she found was a willingness and capability to
perform but inconsistent methods for providing customer service.
Her findings surprised her, for she had assumed that her people
had a mutual understanding about how to do their jobs. As for
her new people, they had worked alongside her experienced people for two weeks or more so they could observe and learn every
facet of the job. "Get it from the horse's mouth" was her training
motto. Besides, she reasoned, that was the way she had learned
her job.

Martha investigated further. The new people had these comments about the training they had received from experienced employees: "Lee was often so busy, he didn't have time to explain
what he was doing." "Ruth knows her job, but she assumed I un-

derstood everything she covered." "Mac was reluctant to let me practice on his customers." Martha concluded that her new people were inadequately trained and that some of her experienced people might also profit from a skills update in view of the company's expansion.

How should we develop the training? Who should do it? When and how should we conduct the training? These were questions Martha had to answer. There were no off-the-shelf programs she could use. She had no training department to rely on. She decided the training was up to her. She reviewed the situation with her boss, who suggested she involve her key people in the training.

Martha went back to her office, closed the door, sat down, and took out a pad and pencil. First, she listed the subjects that she thought needed to be covered. They were:

Customer service responsibilities
Taking customer orders
Filling customer orders
Making customer deliveries
Handling customer complaints

Second, she made assignments for each of the subjects. She took the first subject herself and assigned each of the other subjects to four key people. Third, she decided that the basic content of each subject would be problems and their solutions from the point of view of the customer service representative. Fourth, she felt that all of the subjects could be covered in one day and that the training should be held on a Saturday so her entire staff could be present. She saw no problem with having to pay her people overtime for Saturday work.

Those to whom Martha had assigned subjects had no experience in developing training materials, so she knew she would have to help them with it. She met with each of them for two or three hours and helped them develop permanent reference materials to be distributed during the training. For the subject "Taking customer orders" they developed four one-page handouts:

Handling ten phone problems
Taking phone orders

Using the customer order log
Telephone do's and don'ts

Each subject had a similar format, starting with problems, situations, and challenges faced by the customer service representatives on the job. Well-thought-out solutions followed, along with guidelines for the subject area.

Martha scheduled and held the Saturday training as planned. She and her four key people presented and led discussions in their subject areas. Because of its format, the training appealed to both new and experienced employees. For follow-up, Martha had each location keep a daily chart showing the number of customer complaints by major category such as incomplete order or late delivery. Then she helped her people set and achieve monthly targets for customer service based on getting customer complaints down to mutually agreed levels.

Let's review what happened. At the outset, Martha had relied on OJT to get the performance she wanted. During the company's expansion, this method of training proved inadequate and would have been potentially very expensive, had customers been lost due to the level of customer service provided. During this time, she had −10 performance relative to her responsibility to train. Subsequently, she achieved +10 performance because she accelerated the experience of her entire staff. She enlisted the help of four key people and in one day provided learning that might otherwise have taken days, weeks, or months.

Studies show that supervisors everywhere do very little training beyond OJT. There are several reasons for this.

Why Supervisors Rely Mostly on OJT

- They themselves were trained by OJT.
- They staff primarily with experienced people.
- They have other priorities.
- They have only occasional need to do training.
- They haven't been trained in how to train.
- They wait for training help.
- They lack a training budget.

• *They themselves were trained by OJT.* It's hard to apply something that isn't in one's memory bank. The result is that supervisors tend to emulate those methods by which they themselves were trained. One rationalization they have for this is "Look how good I turned out." However, when used by itself, OJT is slow, costly, and often ineffective. OJT distracts experienced employees from their jobs, causes mistakes to be made by untrained employees, and drags out training time that could otherwise be productive time.

• *They staff primarily with experienced people.* Such an approach works when experienced people are available at competitive compensation levels. However, experienced people still need a certain amount of training, and they do not always have the most potential. Employees who have the most potential are often those without the requisite experience but with the capability to learn quickly and to meet job requirements providing they get effective training.

• *They have other priorities.* OJT is easy to accomplish. You merely pick out somebody who knows how to do the job to teach the new person how to do it. Most supervisors already have full agendas and would rather concentrate their efforts on those activities with which they feel more comfortable or that seem to have more urgency.

• *They have only occasional need to do training.* I can understand why supervisors might rely on OJT if they get only an occasional new person who needs training. However, they are probably overlooking training needs to upgrade the skills of their experienced workers, to develop and install new methods, and to do replacement training for each of their key positions. A sales manager, for example, who is getting so-so results might have the potential to get superior results by upgrading the selling skills of his or her people.

• *They haven't been trained in how to train.* Many people go into training as a career, but this does not mean that a person needs to be a full-time trainer to be effective. At the beginning of this chapter, we saw how simply Martha Merritt developed and conducted training. Any supervisor can do that. Often, all that stands in the way is a psychological hurdle.

• *They wait for training help.* "Our training department hasn't been able to fit us into its schedule, so we continue to rely on OJT"—supervisors who express this view realize there are better ways to do training, but they do not see themselves as initiators of such training. To some degree, they have abrogated to others their responsibility for training.

• *They lack a training budget.* Larger organizations have training departments with budgets; smaller organizations usually do not. Regardless, individual supervisors tend not to have training budgets for off-the-shelf training programs, course and seminar attendance, use of outside resources such as consultants and teachers, audiovisual and video equipment, training facilities, and compensation during training. Consequently, they are reluctant to spend money for such purposes and defer to OJT.

OJT will always be necessary for any complete training program, but its effectiveness can be enhanced immeasurably when supervisors take a number of other training actions. As a supervisor, you are probably most concerned with job training. This means you need to train your new people how to do their jobs; you need to cross-train your experienced people so they know how to do each other's jobs; you need to do replacement training for key positions so that trained replacements are available when needed; you need to train your people in new methods or new technology; and you need to develop and conduct training when you have pressing problems in such areas as quality, safety, and customer service. In addition, today there is a major movement to teach people how to work in teams to improve productivity and support total quality management (TQM). As you may know, TQM is a business process that focuses on customer satisfaction and on continuous improvement in all areas of an organization.

Further, you are probably less interested in educating your people than in training them. I make a distinction between education, which may have little or no application on the job, and training, which has direct application on the job. Education is very necessary to give people knowledge, perspective, and basic skills such as reading, writing, and arithmetic. Schools are in the business of educating more than training, although they do some of both. You need to educate your people sufficiently about your reasons for what you want them to do, but your priority must be training them to do the job. If you want your training to be both economical and effective, I propose you follow this guideline:

Train to do.

This means concentrate your training on the subject matter that your people can use productively. If, for example, you give your people knowledge about the financial workings of your operation, tell them how to use that knowledge. Show them how they can apply it in their individual jobs to increase revenues or to reduce costs.

The optimal amount of training to give your staff is that which will enable them to do their jobs and to realize their individual potential. If you make their learning easy by accelerating their experience, they are likely to become productive much sooner than otherwise and to stay motivated. If you make their learning difficult, they are likely to feel frustrated and to develop don't-care attitudes. You may lose your more qualified people if they become frustrated enough to look for another job.

There are several training subjects common to both production and office employees.

Training Subjects for Production and Office Employees

1. Job description: duties and responsibilities
2. Business function and objectives
3. Customers—external and internal
4. Organization and people
5. Job language and terms
6. Tools and equipment—production, computer systems, networks, telecommunications, others
7. Materials
8. Job methods—knowledge and practice

   - Start-up, operation, shut-down
   - Abnormal situations

9. Performance standards—goals, schedules, budgets
10. Quality requirements
11. Records and reports
12. Health and safety program
13. Housekeeping
14. Union contract compliance
15. Working relationships—internal, with other organizational units, with outside organizations
16. Policies and procedures—work rules, payroll, overtime, customer complaints, improvements ideas, personal prob-

lems, performance review, pay progression, career development, ethical standards, other

Most of these items are self-explanatory, but some bear explanation.

3. *Customers—internal and external.* Every organizational unit has customers. Your people will perform more effectively if they know who your customers are and how they should be treated. Recently, I had lunch with a customer of one of my clients. She told me about some of the problems she had in getting the products and services that she wanted from my client, but what really irritated her was the new receptionist, who treated her like a stranger. Beyond this, she was upset that my client's management had neglected to train the receptionist about who she was. Customers want to be treated like customers. This goes for internal customers as well. Maintenance people serve production people. Production people serve salespeople. Computer people serve those who use computer services. Accounting people serve those who use and provide accounting data. Engineers serve users of engineering services. If you train your people accordingly, you and your people will make a much larger contribution to your organization than otherwise.

5. *Job language and terms.* Tourists who go to a foreign country tend to feel insecure when they do not know the local language. New employees feel this way, even those who come from other organizations within your industry. You can enhance your training by spending time on the language you use.

8. *Job methods—knowledge and practice.* As a prelude to on-the-job practice, your people will learn their jobs more readily if you provide them with written how-to's. Use your key people to help you develop such write-ups for each facet of each job. Note the separate provision for abnormal situations. What should your people do when their equipment breaks down, or when materials are not available, or when quality problems develop, or when specified procedures don't work, or when other departments don't do their jobs, or when customers complain? You and your staff can predict at least 80 percent of the abnormal situations. Develop and conduct related training, and you will do more to help your people feel in control of their jobs than any other training action you can take.

There are many different kinds of selling, but one of the most challenging is the kind done by outside salespeople who make calls on customers and prospects to sell products and services. One way or another, these people learn about the products and services they have to sell as well as the industry in which they work. Except for those in larger organizations, relatively few of them get any training in selling beyond that of an occasional outside sales trainer who has a generic message. This can be helpful, but it doesn't hold a candle to the potential value of your own custom-tailored program in selling skills. There are several subjects that you might deal with as they pertain to your products or services and to your customers.

Selling Subjects for Outside Salespeople

Your selling job
Why buyers buy
Dealing with buyer differences
Selling through your personal strengths
Strategic territory analysis and planning
Solution selling methods
Questioning and listening techniques
Planning and making sales calls
Competitive analysis and response
Using people resources and sales tools
Prospecting methods
Overcoming sales objections and retardants
Selling through the written word
Proposal development and presentation
Phone selling techniques
Negotiating methods
Creative selling techniques
Group selling methods
Sales career development
Time management

I have found that individuals with superior selling skills and only adequate product knowledge will far outperform individuals with superior product knowledge and only adequate selling skills. I don't mean to downplay the amount of knowledge your salespeople need about your products and services, but I do mean to suggest that your salespeople may perform significantly better with improved salesmanship. You may need to rely on your training department or outside resources to develop and conduct such training. On the other hand, your salespeople may be the only resource you need if you solicit their support, make assignments, and help them develop and conduct their own training.

When you train your people, you show them you care. The obvious question then is: How much caring do they need?

I like the thinking of Peter M. Senge, a researcher at Massachusetts Institute of Technology who promotes the concept of the learning organization. He says an organization should continually expand its capacity to create its own future. Otherwise, it becomes a victim of slow, gradual processes to which it is 90 percent blind. To support his contention, he observes that few of our corporations live beyond the age of forty. We jeopardize our futures if we rely only on what has worked in the past.

If these ideas make sense to you, then all working people have a continual need for training. You're not in business just to do training, but you are in business to provide your people with sufficient training to meet both the current and the future needs of your organization.

To begin effective training for your area of responsibility, I recommend you follow seven guidelines.

Training Guidelines

1. Establish training priority.
2. Develop the training.
3. Conduct the training.
4. Promote application on the job.
5. Measure training results.
6. Train subsequent employees.
7. Repeat the process.

1. *Establish training priority.* You probably have ideas about your department's most important training needs. You may be right about them, but your training will be more effective if you validate your ideas among those affected—your staff, your management, and your internal and external customers.

Suppose your controller says to you, "We've got to figure out a way to reduce overtime. Our labor costs are breaking budget, and your data input personnel are contributing to the problem." What would you do? One alternative is to develop ways to improve data input procedures and then announce to your staff that you're going to train them in ways that will eliminate delays and be more efficient. Another alternative is to validate among your staff members and others affected the need for improvement procedures before you do so. Maybe your staff sees overtime as a way to increase their pay, or maybe they feel they're due their fair share of overtime because other departments get it. If you can alleviate either or both of these problems, maybe you have higher training needs, such as how your staff can interpret the data as they input it. For example, they may be able to provide early-warning signals for emerging problems with other departments or customers.

A more orderly approach to determining your training needs by priority is to make an occasional survey among those affected—especially in connection with any annual planning that you may do. Then you can integrate training with your other planned activities. To establish your training priority, give weight to that training that will have the greatest dollar impact in revenue or cost savings.

2. *Develop the training.* The person who has the most credibility is the one who is doing it successfully. That's why I prefer to have you rely on your people as your most important training resource—providing they have adequate knowledge and skills among them. Use the problem-solution format discussed earlier, and they can be effective whether or not they have prior training experience. See that how-to-do-it key points get put in writing so your people will have permanent reference. People learn better when you combine hearing and seeing. Blackboard and chalk or chart paper and marker are probably your best training aids, but don't overlook the potential of videotape or computerized learning to bring operations or customer applications right into the training room. Doing provides the best learning, so make provision for adequate practice in the training room or on the job. Don't forget to cover abnormal situations.

The easiest way to develop training is with the resources you already have. This includes tapping the talents of anyone in your organization, including top management. However, there will be times when you need outside expertise—when, for example, you want to introduce new methods or technology. Don't shy away from the money this will cost, whether or not it's in your budget. If you have done a good job of establishing your training priority, you should be able to justify your training plans to your management.

3. *Conduct the training.* Your mind can only absorb what your seat can endure. Remember this when you schedule your training. Two hours a week for four weeks is sometimes better than a full day of training or two half days of training. Make sure your training facilities are conducive to learning even if you have to spend money on outside facilities. When possible, conduct the training during business hours. This will communicate to your people the value you put on the training. Provide a training atmosphere where you share ideas and where everyone can contribute to the learning.

4. *Promote application on the job.* It is much harder to apply training on the job than it is in the training room. Old habits and other priorities get in the way. So you must follow up with your people over a period of days, weeks, or months, depending on the amount of change or improvement you are trying to accomplish. Remember to brief those affected who may not have had the training. Your workers may need the support of other employees and your management if, for example, you are changing the way orders are to be processed.

5. *Measure training results.* You have developed and conducted the training, and you have achieved the intended results. This will be obvious to all interested parties. Right? Wrong. Others, including your management, have their own agendas, and they may question the time and money you invested in the training. Measure the training results with both subjective and objective data. Get ratings and opinions about the training from your staff and from those affected. Calculate dollar results relating to improved revenue, reduced waste, improved safety, increased efficiency, improved on-time deliveries, fewer quality defects, shorter processing time, reduced customer complaints, and the like. Summarize the data on a sheet of paper, and report it to those whose support you will need for future training.

6. *Train subsequent employees.* New employees who join your group will be at a training disadvantage unless you make provision for them. One way is to give each of them a copy of the train-

ing materials, supplemented with a one-on-one review by you or by those who conducted the training. Another way is to give each of them an audio- or videotape of the training for their review and study.

7. *Repeat the process.* If you support the concept of the learning organization, your department will have continuing learning or training needs. As before, establish your training priority and follow the steps that have given you successful training results in the past.

If you were not certain how to approach training at the beginning of this chapter, I hope you realize that you can do effective training without being a training specialist. Any effort you exert to give your group further training is likely to be an improvement and have beneficial economic results. Further, when your workers can accelerate their experience through training, they increase their own potential as well as that of your organization. And you? You have training needs also—to continue to improve your effectiveness as a supervisor. For example, you may want to learn about self-directed work teams where supervisors function as team leaders who empower their team members to satisfy customers. One way for you to get ideas about how to improve is to take an occasional course or seminar. Another way is to read and study—including the book you now have before you: *Superior Supervision.*

9

Motivate

+10 PERFORMANCE: Motivate according to their needs
−10 PERFORMANCE: Motivate according to your needs

Are you aware that:

What motivates you—money, recognition, opportunity—may not motivate all of your people?

One of my clients has a commercial copying operation. A while back, the supervisor of the copying department found on his desk an unsigned poem. Here is the poem, modified to change the names of individuals and to include identifications of certain people's positions in brackets:

Ode to a Trimmer

I'm a trimmer
And I hate it
'Cause it makes me
Feel degraded.

Trim the copy
On the shadow
All this trimming
Makes me mad-o

Keep the margin
On the left
The machine noise
Makes me deaf.

That guy Crocker [supervisor]
He's a jerk

'Cause he gives us
Lots of work.

Trim those well logs
Nice and neat
Stamp all over them
With my feet.

Raise the blade
Then push it down
Up again and
Then back down.

It sure would be great
To be home instead
Doing this action
In my bed.

Work all day
In the hardest way
For the least
Amount of pay.

Inflation
Scared of lay-offs
Where is Joanne [another employee]
Took the day off.

Here is Crocker
Trimmer power
Twenty-five dollars
He gets per hour.

Time to go home
Please stay late
Oh Jim Crocker
It's you we hate.

And while this day
I'm already hating
Here comes Baker [counter salesperson]
With another [customer] waiting.

> What keeps us going
> Is our idol
> Hooray for Ginny [disabled employee]
> The queen of might-all!!

What does this poem say to you? To me, it says the trimmer is not very happy and has significant untapped potential. Also, it tells me that supervisor Jim Crocker is unaware of or indifferent to the motivational needs of this trimmer. Why might this be so?

If Jim Crocker is happy and motivated in his job, he probably feels the trimmer should be too. Or Jim may have been a trimmer earlier in his career, saw opportunity, did a good job, got promoted, and today feels that same opportunity exists for his trimmer. In either case, Jim would be assuming that what motivates or motivated him also motivates his trimmer. How valid is such an assumption?

As human beings, we all have common needs, such as for food, clothing, shelter, transportation, recreation, acceptance, and recognition. Satisfying these needs is a common motivation. But— and it's a big *but*—we also have motivational differences. There are differences that depend on our age, heredity, upbringing, values, education, career progress, marital status, health, and a host of other factors. So, for example, if I am your supervisor, it is not very likely that what motivates me most importantly today is also what motivates you most importantly today. Yet unless I stop and think, I am very likely to project my own motivations onto you. To some degree, I will be right, but to a larger degree, I will probably be wrong.

Harry Lennox is president of a manufacturing company that has about three hundred employees. Recently his employees voted on whether to have a union represent them. Harry was surprised that the employees were considering such representation, because he felt his firm had always been more than fair with them and offered wages, benefits, and job security comparable to the best in his industry. The vote was close, but the employees voted not to have union representation at that time. Harry knows about other firms that function very effectively with unions; however, he and his management team would prefer not to have a union and were relieved when the voting result was announced. They were still left with a problem, though: how to prevent successful unionization efforts in the future.

Within a week or two after the vote, Harry received this unsigned letter:

Dear Mr. Lennox:

Thank you very much for all the increased benefits on our health plan.

I am very glad the union didn't come in during the election we had recently. Next year they probably will try again. I have a few suggestions that may help keep them out.

It seems to me that a lot of the problems that we had with the union were related to employee dissatisfaction with wages and benefits—obviously. But I think another factor should be investigated—the supervisory staff in all departments. There had been and still is a lot of shop talk about how supervisors are insensitive to the feelings and needs of employees. Frustrations build up because employees are treated this way, with nowhere to turn to. I think a lot of the supervisors do this because there is really no one to really keep an eye on them; there is no grading system for them.

Since employees get reviewed by the supervisors, why not let the employees of each department grade their supervisors? This, of course, would be confidential. The reason I suggest this is that employees have no way to vent any grievances they may have, or for that matter, no way to praise supervisors to you. Of course there are drawbacks to this system—such as accuracy of the surveys—but I think you will at least get a good idea where potential problems may arise in certain departments. I believe a lot of people in the company voted union because they were mad at how they were treated and not given good pay for good work. According to shop talk, this has been happening for a long time, even before there was union talk.

I would have the following items in the survey grading the supervisors. Of course, you may want to add more if you like my idea. On a scale of 0 to 5, I suggest the following factors be rated.

1. Honesty with employees
2. Leadership ability
3. Respect for employees (courtesy)
4. Does supervisor communicate clearly ideas and directions about jobs?
5. Knowledge of his or her trade or profession
6. Is supervisor receptive to new ideas from employees?

7. Is supervisor creative with new ideas to improve the department?
8. Is supervisor pleasant to work with? If no, please explain.
9. What would you do or change in your department if you were the supervisor?
10. How satisfied are you with your supervisor?

Results could then be tabulated and used by you to judge how your supervisors are doing.

If you decide to use this idea, it will accomplish three things:

1. Help employees to vent any complaints directly to your attention.
2. Supervisors will be less prone to be "power crazy" if they know they will be accountable to you through the employees.
3. You can directly mediate any friction between employee and supervisor by correcting any possible misconduct by either side. By doing so, you will stop tension from building up again into talk about unions.

Reviews could be taken twice a year. If a supervisor were to get continual low marks for a period of time, that would indicate possible change or corrective action on your part.

My other suggestion is this: Please don't lose touch with us workers. A lot of us want to know that you care and that you want to listen to us. I am just another worker but I care about the people and I don't want the union to come in if we can stop it by the idea I have.

Thank you for your time.

Harry read and reread the letter. He concluded that his supervisors were not in touch with all of the needs of their people and that employee feedback on supervisory performance might be a good idea. He explored the idea with his department heads, who in turn did so with their supervisors.

The supervisors felt that their performance should not be the only factor evaluated. They felt other factors should also be evaluated, such as job assignments, pay, benefits, policies, procedures, employee cooperation, training, opportunity, and top management performance. Harry and his department heads decided the supervisors were right. So he asked his human resources supervisor to develop and conduct an anonymous opinion-and-suggestion survey among all employees.

The survey results showed that several areas needed improvement, but the employees' main concern was for improvement in supervisory performance—just as the anonymous letter had suggested. The supervisors were reported to be so production-oriented that they tended not to be concerned with individual employee needs, some of which were expressed. One employee had a long commute that needed resolution. A second employee had work hours that caused family problems. A third employee was bored with his work and impatient to get ahead. A fourth employee had an ambition outside the company and was interested only in working a couple of years while she saved some money.

Harry and his department heads held departmental meetings to share the survey results and to get further input. Then they developed and announced plans for meeting the more important needs. To improve supervisory performance, they decided on three actions:

1. Ask supervisors to hold individual meetings with their workers to identify and help resolve any pressing individual concerns.
2. Conduct a supervisory training program to improve supervisory skills and learn ways to motivate employees.
3. Implement an annual performance review program, wherein supervisors and employees can exchange constructive input about each other's performance and concerns—with emphasis on any unfilled motivational needs of employees.

The jury isn't in yet on how well Harry and his management team will follow through. But if they do a good job, I predict Harry's company will remain union-free.

Supervisors who are primarily people-oriented find it easier to be sensitive to their workers' motivational needs than supervisors who are primarily production-oriented. And production-oriented superdoers (outstanding individual performers) are the ones who often get promoted into supervisory positions. As supervisors, they continue to be more production-oriented than people-oriented, and they tend to assume what motivates them motivates others.

Whether you are primarily people-oriented or production-oriented, you can make wrong assumptions about what motivates your people. How can you avoid doing so?

First, it's helpful to know what psychologists and other behavioral scientists have learned about motivating employees in general. Second, it's helpful to explore what might motivate an individual employee at a given point in time.

Three behavioral scientists who have made major contributions in the field of employee motivation are Abraham Maslow, Frederick Herzberg, and M. Scott Myers. Let's review some of their key concepts.

Abraham Maslow developed a theory of the hierarchy of human needs. At the bottom of the hierarchy are physical needs, such as for food, clothing, shelter, and sex. Next is the need for security, such as freedom from physical or mental harm. Next is the need for love or belonging, indicated, for example, by one's desire to like and be liked by others. Next is the need for status, such as for self-respect and recognition by others. At the top of the hierarchy is the need for self-actualization—realization of personal potential. People's physical needs come first. When they are met, security becomes important; then love or belonging; then status; and then self-actualization. When lower-level needs are met, meeting higher-level needs has greater motivational potential.

Frederick Herzberg recommends motivating employees through job enrichment. He identifies dissatisfiers, such as pay, hours, policies, administration, supervision, working conditions, and interpersonal relationships. When you eliminate the dissatisfiers, you don't make people happy, but you keep people from being unhappy. Motivators are responsibility, interesting work, achievement, recognition, and opportunity to grow and advance. Motivators can be used to enrich jobs. But job enrichment is not the same thing as job enlargement, where an employee merely has more of similar work to do. Job enrichment helps employees use more of their talents and work up to their potential.

M. Scott Myers developed the jellybean theory of motivation. To explain it, he describes a tourist driving through a national park. The tourist sees a bear, rolls down his window, and offers the bear a jellybean. The bear eats the jellybean but does not go away. The tourist offers the bear more and more jellybeans, until his bag is empty. The bear doesn't understand the empty bag, gets angry, pulls the tourist from the car, and eats him. Question: Is this a bad bear? The answer is no. The bear is analogous to the employee who will always accept more pay, benefits, or improved working conditions. But that willingness does not mean such goodies are motivators. Rather, jellybeans like pay and benefits are maintenance factors. They must be competitive, but they do not offer motivation. Motivation results from factors such as growth, achievement, responsibility, and recognition relating to the work itself.

Here is a way to summarize the ideas of Maslow, Herzberg, and Myers:

Employees used to say, *treat* me well.
Today they say, *use* me well.

Motivational theories apply to employees in general. They may not apply fully to a particular individual at a particular point in time. An individual may be motivated to perform or to stay on the job for one or a combination of factors. We can classify such factors under these headings:

Nature of job
Tangible compensation
Intangible compensation
Job environment
Personal factors

An employee can feel motivated or demotivated based primarily on one or more factors relating to the nature of his or her job.

Motivational Factors Relating to Nature of Job

- Duties, responsibilities, authority
- Job title
- Reporting relationship
- Resources
- Work hours
- Training program
- Confidence in supervisor
- Confidence in upper management
- Budget size
- Level of travel
- Planning methods
- Goals program
- Control methods
- Performance evaluation program

Very few people will work for nothing, so *tangible compensation* can be either a motivator or demotivator. Tangible compensation takes many forms.

Motivational Factors Relating to Tangible Compensation

Regular pay
Overtime opportunity
Incentive program
Layoff policy
Compensation review program
Medical benefits program
Disability income program
Time off and leave program
Automobile policy
Expense account policy
Vacation and holiday program
Childcare program
Retirement program
Deferred compensation program
Moving expense policy
Life insurance program
Membership program
Trips and conferences
Educational assistance
Discounts on products or services
Ownership opportunity
Termination program

An employee whose pay relates directly to his or her performance—as in commission, bonus, and other incentive programs—will generally be motivated by pay. An older employee may be more interested in a retirement program than a younger employee. A young married employee may be interested mostly in the medical benefits program or the childcare program. An employee who is asked to move from one assignment to another may be most interested in the moving expense policy. I know some salespeople who stay motivated even though their regular pay is at the low end of the competitive scale. Reason: They are treated royally at periodic sales conferences in resort locations.

Behavioral scientists have helped us understand how *intangible compensation* can affect employee motivation.

Motivational Factors Relating to Intangible Compensation

Use of talent or ability
Sense of accomplishment
Acceptance of ideas
Trust
Independence
Feeling of inclusion
Internal recognition—within employee's organization
Public recognition—outside employee's organization
Personal development opportunity
Advancement potential
Job security
Recreational program
Counseling program

Except for the last two items, this list contains factors that have been promoted by behavioral scientists. These factors are also appeals in employee empowerment programs, which seek to tap the potential of employees at all levels. While probably not as important as the other items listed, recreational and counseling programs can be strong motivators for certain individuals. For example, some employees are motivated by participation in an employer-sponsored sports team such as softball, basketball, or bowling. Other employees appreciate the sometimes life-saving help given them through employer-provided counseling for chemical dependency, personal financial management, or many other personal issues.

Job environment factors can have a major impact on employee motivation.

Motivational Factors Relating to Job Environment

Equal opportunity
Stress level
Personal work relationships
Physical environment
Safety program

Unionization
Union-management cooperation
Work rules
Disciplinary program
Grievance procedure
Geographical location
Type of industry
Size of organization
Mission of organization
Strategy of organization
Performance of organization

The last three items may need a word of explanation. Today we hear about the need for shared vision among all employees in an organization. The mission of an organization—to serve a cause, to achieve prominence, to create a new industry, or to make it affordable to everybody—can be a strong motivator. The strategy an organization uses to accomplish its mission can be motivating—through new technology, use of new methods of distribution, reliance on employee teams, and expansion to new markets. Most of us like to be part of a winning team, so the performance of the organization as a whole can be a strong motivator.

The most powerful motivators can be *personal factors*.

Motivational Factors Relating to Personal Factors

Fear of failure
Fear of disappointing others
Fear of disciplinary action
Fear of authority
Sense of loyalty
Outside obligations
Outside interests
Ambition—internal or external

Among these personal factors, supervisors should rely on the positive motivators. But if they don't work, supervisors may have to resort to the negative motivators, as suggested by the first four items. Probably because of their temperaments, upbringing, or prior work environment, some employees are motivated more by fear than by positive motivators. Other employees have an abiding sense of loyalty, outside obligations such as to dependent family members, or outside interests such as religious activities, or community involvement, or even hobbies. Lastly, ambition can be one's dominant motivator. Not everyone has a defined ambition, but many people do—whether for the short range, long range, or both. Internal ambition might be for position, pay, achievement, recognition, job location, or retirement. External ambition might be for home purchase, children's educations, hobby or sports achievement, travel, further education, net worth, or even another career.

Now you may wonder, "Am I expected to memorize all of these factors and try to apply them in motivating my people?" The answer is no. What you must have is a keen awareness that there are many motivational factors and that what motivates a particular employee today may differ from what motivates him or her tomorrow.

Throughout this chapter, I've tried to make clear that your biggest temptation will be to treat your people as if their motivational needs are the same as yours. That is the way to have −10 performance relative to your responsibility to motivate. By contrast, the way to have +10 performance is to identify and help your people meet *their* motivational needs.

Although I refer to "your" responsibility to motivate, you can't really motivate anyone. You can't force a person to want to work or to do good work—not for very long, anyway. People take jobs because they need to work. Then it's largely up to you to take those actions that create the conditions that cause each of them to become and stay motivated, from within themselves. With this premise, let's consider guidelines to meet the motivational needs of employees generally and of individual employees.

Motivating Guidelines

A. Employees *generally* will respond to these actions:
1. Empower them.
2. Expect performance.
3. Give them meaningful recognition.
4. Train them and encourage self-development.

B. *Individual* employees will respond to these actions:
1. Ask each employee, "What do you want from your job?"
2. Help each employee to meet his or her needs for both short and long range.

There are four actions you can take that will get favorable response from your people *in general.*

1. *Empower them.* Delegate responsibility and enrich jobs. Give your people as much responsibility and decision-making responsibility as possible. Let them plan, schedule, and inspect their own work. Let them incur costs, within established boundaries. Give them the authority to settle complaints and to issue credits. Develop mutually agreed rules and controls, but keep them to a minimum. Ask your people to develop and try out improvements. Consider letting them develop their own budgets and deal directly with customers and vendors. General George S. Patton once said, "Never tell people how to do things. Tell them what you want them to achieve, and they will surprise you with their ingenuity." When more than one department is involved, such as with order processing, establish self-managed multifunctional teams to make improvements. Ask your people to make continuing improvements, a major premise of Total Quality Management.

When you delegate responsibility and enrich jobs, you empower your people, and they feel more in control. Then the employees tend to feel that they *own* their jobs. Most people value and take better care of the things they own. (See Chapters 3 and 11 for more complete discussions about how to delegate and improve.)

2. *Expect performance.* Perhaps you're familiar with psychologist Douglas McGregor's Theory X and Theory Y styles of management. If you believe in Theory X, you feel people are lazy, need watching, and have to be prodded. If you believe in Theory Y, you believe people seek responsibility and are capable of self-control. In practice, each style becomes a self-fulfilling prophecy. In other words, you get what you expect. I am reminded of the physics professor who used to tell each new class that 50 percent of them would fail because the class was so hard. Sure enough, that's what happened year after year. Then he decided to try an experiment. He told the new class that they were unusually bright and that all of them would pass. Sure enough, all of them passed, even though the professor used the same testing procedures.

3. *Give them meaningful recognition.* Everyone wants to feel important. Seek the input of your people on those matters that affect them. Praise them or their work only when you mean it. Avoid

using praise as the introduction to an unwanted assignment. Create a formal recognition program, such as The President's Club or The 100 Percent Club. Publicize unusual achievement. Encourage innovators to give talks or to write for publications.

These are typical comments employees have made to me in organizations that don't realize the motivational value of meaningful recognition: "My paycheck is the only recognition I get." "We don't get praise, but we get hell." "If they praised us, they figure they'd have to pay us more." "Because we're professionals, we're expected to do good work. If they gave us praise, I guess they'd feel they were treating us as children." "If we got outside recognition, they'd worry about losing us to competitors."

4. *Train them and encourage self-development.* The increased use of computers, the application of new technologies, and the introduction of new management methods such as those we've learned from the Japanese have changed many jobs and will continue to do so. To ensure that your people stay qualified, encourage them to develop themselves through courses, seminars, reading, and participation in community and professional organizations. In addition, you have a responsibility to train. Develop and conduct training to introduce new methods, solve quality problems, improve customer service, and the like. Do cross-training, so your people learn each other's jobs. Do succession-training, so you have a trained replacement for each key job. (See Chapter 8 for a more complete discussion of training.)

Now let's discuss those motivational actions you can take with your people as *individuals*.

1. *Ask each employee, "What do you want from your job?* To find out an individual's needs:

Just ask!

You can do so formally, by scheduling and holding a meeting with each of your staff members at least once a year. You can do so informally throughout the year, by taking the initiative yourself when you see a motivational problem or by responding to employee initiative. Your awareness of the broad range of individual motivational factors discussed earlier in this chapter will help you draw out what your employee may be thinking or feeling.

2. *Help each employee to meet his or her needs for both the short and the long range.* Identifying an employee's motivational needs and doing something about them are two distinct challenges. In other words, your follow-through is critical. If Clint wants more pay, for example, make clear to him the specific quantity and quality of performance he must achieve or the skills he must develop in order to get more pay. You may have to arrange training or provide periodic counsel to him. If Fran wants the opportunity to replace you some day, avoid any temptation to discourage her; rather, help her develop a written personal development program that she can implement over a period of time, perhaps a year or two. Your follow-through actions for your people are as varied as their individual needs. You can't even assume cash is the appropriate contest reward. One sales manager found that every one of his people wanted a reward in the form of department store gift certificates, so they would avoid spending cash on routine household needs.

I hope you don't feel you have to be a psychologist to be a good motivator—to help your employees motivate themselves. It's pretty much a matter of treating them as you'd like to be treated. If you tend not to be people-oriented or if your own bosses haven't treated you this way in the past, you may have a bigger challenge than otherwise. But the payoff is in employee performance and in the satisfaction you feel from enhancing your skill in *Superior Supervision.*

10

Counsel

+10 PERFORMANCE: Act on early-warning signs
−10 PERFORMANCE: Let crises develop

Are you aware that:

You can be more influential in helping your
people identify and meet their personal or
career crises than anyone else on earth?

Judy Jenkins is programming supervisor in the information
technology department of a large utility. She supervises a staff
of ten. A few months ago, she noticed that Dave, one of her pro-
grammers, began to miss some deadlines. He called in sick three
or four times and then wasn't able to make up the time. She wondered if he was feeling stress, so she met with him. Dave told her
not to worry, that stress was not a problem, and that he'd do better.

During the next couple of months, Dave's performance was excellent both in quantity and quality of output. Then he began to
call in sick again. Judy decided to analyze his record of absences
from the time he was hired. She found that Monday absences pre-
vailed. "Could that be significant?" she wondered. She reviewed
the matter with her boss, who validated her concern and referred
her to the company's human resources director.

Within a couple of days she met with the human resources director, who observed that a pattern of long weekends sometimes
indicates a dependency problem—on alcohol or other chemicals.
Judy asked what she could do in Dave's case. The human resources director told her that there was probably nothing she
could do at this point unless Dave's job performance were clearly
affected. What Dave did outside work was strictly his own business.

Judy resigned herself to the advice she got, but she did talk to Dave again about his absences. She asked him if there were any work-related causes to his absence. He said no. Then she told him about his pattern of Monday absences. That did it. Dave blew his cool. "What are you getting at?" he demanded.

Judy asked Dave to meet with her in a private conference room in about ten minutes. Then she went back to her office to organize her thoughts. Dave showed up for the meeting, which he began with an apology. Judy accepted it but went on to say that she felt she had hit a raw nerve and that Dave's response was not typical of his normal behavior. She explained that she was concerned about him, that something must be bothering him, and that maybe there was something she could do to help.

Dave made no response for about a minute. Then tears welled up in his eyes. He said there was nothing she could do. Then they both sat there in silence. Finally Judy asked if Dave would do her a favor and go see his doctor. He said he didn't really have one. Judy responded by offering to help him find someone through the company. Further, she assured him that any discussions between him and the doctor would be completely confidential. Dave seemed open to her offer, so she called the human resources director, got a recommendation for a doctor, and gave the information to Dave. Dave said he would call for an appointment, and Judy said she'd follow up with him in a week or so to make sure he was able to get the appointment.

Within a month, Dave asked for a thirty-day leave. Judy wanted to know the reason. Dave hesitated, then explained that he wanted to enter a treatment program. He told her that the doctor to whom she had referred him had put him in touch with a specialist who helped him realize he had an alcohol problem. He had gotten to the point where he could admit the problem, but he needed treatment. Judy suggested that he probably wanted a prompt approval for the leave. He nodded appreciatively, and Judy said she understood. Then she offered him her support and said his job would be waiting for him when he returned to work.

Sometimes that's all that it takes—a little push—to help an employee take a life-saving action. Other times the challenge is much bigger and takes much longer. In either case, you are in a unique position to help an employee with a pressing personal or career problem. Here's why:

You observe your employees and get frequent input about them over a long period of time.

You have economic leverage on them—a certain amount of control over their livelihood.

No one else on earth is in this position. The extent to which you have and accept this realization will probably be reflected in the amount of counseling you do.

I've interviewed thousands of supervisors in the course of my consulting. Often I ask them what they think their personal strengths are. Usually I get responses like technical knowledge, problem-solving ability, or skill in dealing with people. I was surprised recently when one supervisor told me that her counseling skill was one of her major strengths. I asked why she felt that way. She said, "I've had excellent help through counseling, and I want to pass it on. People tell me I'm effective and that I have a calming effect on them." I wish I could clone her and place her as a model among supervisors everywhere to help them realize their potential in counseling. I find that most supervisors neglect or avoid counseling, beyond what they have to do as a routine performance or pay review. There are several reasons.

Why Supervisors Don't Counsel Their People

- They lack awareness of their responsibility to counsel.
- They're not held accountable.
- They avoid opportunities.
- They've never been counseled.
- They do coaching instead of counseling.

• *They lack awareness of their responsibility to counsel.* Some supervisors recognize their responsibility to counsel their people, whether or not it is reflected in the written job description. Other supervisors do not recognize their responsibility to counsel. Unless supervisors have a clear understanding of such responsibility, they are unlikely to do much counseling.

• *They're not held accountable.* Supervisors can have counseling responsibility—it can even be in the job description—but it does not really exist unless there's accountability. Accountability exists only if the supervisor is evaluated on counseling performance during pay review. Supervisors can get help in counseling from human resources people or an outside professional, but the responsibility must rest with them.

• *They avoid opportunities.* Are you familiar with the term *pro forma compliance?* It means to do only what you have to do to get by. Supervisors comply pro forma when they do only the counseling required of them. Many organizations require supervisors at all levels to do performance and pay reviews with their direct reports. Usually a review of either type—sometimes they're combined—is conducted in a private meeting where the supervisor counsels an employee about how to maintain and improve performance. As effective as such counseling might be, supervisors miss the boat if their counseling stops there. Employees have counseling needs at other times, and the supervisor can play a critical role. Inadequate counseling skill and confidence can be roadblocks, however.

• *They're never been counseled.* Many supervisors have never had meaningful counseling themselves—perhaps because they never felt the need for it. So it is unlikely that they can appreciate fully the value of effective counseling. Where do you think such supervisors put counseling on their list of supervisory priorities? If it is on their list at all, it is at or near the bottom.

• *They do coaching instead of counseling.* Hallway counseling occurs when a supervisor counsels an employee when they are both standing in a high-traffic location, such as a hallway or sales floor. In other words, the supervisor gives little time or attention to a major concern of an employee. Often a supervisor can do effective coaching this way: "Why don't you call Jeff?" "I'd confirm the specs." "See if you can get a time extension." All supervisors do this kind of coaching—usually in connection with an employee's work. But subjects of a serious and personal nature require privacy, listening, patience, and time. That's what effective counseling provides.

When supervisors don't counsel their people in a timely and effective manner, crises can develop. Examples of these crises are:

• A minor problem of tardiness and absence becomes a major problem.
• Inattention, causing minor quality problems, develops into a preoccupation, causing major quality problems.

- Several minor complaints from customers turn into major complaints and lost revenue.
- A series of minor illnesses becomes a major illness.
- Several minor accidents turn into a major accident.
- Sexual innuendo grows into a sexual harassment lawsuit.
- Minor work-rule offenses develop into a major infraction.
- Minor disagreements develop into major conflicts, even violence.

Supervisors can often prevent crises through counseling, if they are sensitive to and act on early-warning signs.

Early-Warning Signs Indicating a Need for Counseling

- Waning job performance
- Deteriorating attitude
- Declining attendance
- Accumulating infractions of work rules
- Worsening relations with others
- Growing inattention
- Decreasing tolerance for stress
- Increasing proneness to accidents
- Increasing intake of stimulants or medication
- Increasing frequency and seriousness of illness

All supervisors observe such signs when they occur and take corrective action, such as coaching, disciplining, or training. But not all supervisors do counseling as a separate and distinct corrective action. How about you? Counseling can help your employees do better work, solve a personal problem, or realize their ambition in more ways than you may imagine.

Ways That Counseling Can Help Employees

A. Do better work
  - Quantity of output
  - Quality of performance
  - Customer satisfaction
  - Cost reduction
  - Interpersonal relationships
  - Work-rule compliance
  - Safety compliance
  - Innovation

- Acceptance of change
- Acceptance of disciplinary action
- Acceptance of performance appraisal
- Acceptance of pay adjustment

B. Solve a personal problem
- Domestic or personal relationship
- Financial management
- Chemical dependency
- Physical health
- Stress management
- Control of self-defeating behavior
- Mental health
- Discrimination
- Sexual harassment
- Legal action

C. Realize ambition
- Pay
- Responsibility
- Recognition
- Job security
- Personal development
- Family desire
- Other career
- Retirement
- Outplacement

It's quite a list, isn't it? Maybe even an intimidating one. "How can I be expert in all of these areas?" you may be thinking. "I'd have to go to school the rest of my life to give qualified counseling in each subject area." Not really.

First of all, you are expert—or on your way to becoming one—in your work area. As a supervisor, you have responsibility to help your staff perform and, when appropriate, to help them do better work. Second, you don't have to be expert in how to solve each person's personal problems. Even if you have solved a personal problem for yourself, your personal solution may not apply to or be best for your employee. All you have to do is help your people identify the need for and get qualified counsel.

Third, you have some expertise about how to realize ambition within your own organization, in that you hold a position to which one or more of your people may aspire. Beyond that, you have access to other resources, such as your boss or someone in human resources, who can provide help to aspiring individuals either directly or through you. Chances are you can help meet most of your employees' career needs over the next year or two through coaching, training, committee or team assignments, and through planned self-development, such as taking outside courses, reading, and participating in community and professional organizations. What is critical is that you are supportive and do not stand in an employee's way. You can even help employees whom you are terminating, through outplacement counseling, which will help them find a new position.

We've reviewed your responsibility, your opportunity, and your potential for counseling. Now, how do you go about counseling.

Counseling Guidelines

1. Act on early-warning signs.
2. Initiate or welcome counseling opportunities.
3. Hold a thirty-to-sixty-minute meeting in a location conducive to helping the employee.
4. Invite or present pertinent facts and opinions.
5. Listen with your head and heart, then play it back.
6. Explore alternative solutions.
7. Help the employee decide who will do what by when.
8. Follow up to ensure implementation of planned action.

1. *Act on early-warning signs.* Early-warning signs accumulate and evolve; one or two alone don't usually presage an impending crisis. At some point, however, you must decide to act—to initiate a counseling meeting. If you're not sure what that point is, get input from those of your workers who will be open with you and are concerned about helping Abe or Rita. Also, talk to your peers or your boss, who may have relevant experience. They'll help you decide whether you have a temporary or a growing problem.

2. *Initiate or welcome counseling opportunities.* To address the early-warning signs or with a routine performance or pay review, initiate the counseling. At other times, be sensitive and receptive

to any initiative taken by an employee to talk to you about an important personal concern. If Chong asks about his future with your organization, he may really be saying he's thinking of leaving or is entertaining an outside offer. If Sonja comments about not being able to get ahead, she may feel she's being discriminated against. If Everett complains about how difficult it is to make ends meet, he may be in personal financial difficulty. If Patricia describes an unmanageable juvenile, she may be having a domestic problem. Such remarks don't necessarily indicate a serious personal problem, so proceed cautiously. Your main criteria for inviting an employee to sit down and talk is that the employee seems very concerned or that the employee's performance has been affected. You're not in the hand-holding business, but you are in business to ensure the performance of your people and to help your organization keep good people.

3. *Hold a thirty-to-sixty-minute meeting in a location conducive to helping the employee.* Effective counseling takes time, so don't try to fit it in just before lunch or the end of the work period. Do counseling when you can be reasonably relaxed and unhurried. Allow at least thirty minutes to establish rapport and to follow the remaining guidelines. Schedule additional meeting(s) if necessary. Make sure the location is private, not in a fishbowl atmosphere where the employee will feel observed. If you lack the right facility, go off-site—say, for a cup of coffee or tea. Avoid combining food with counseling unless you want your employee to have indigestion.

4. *Invite or present pertinent facts and opinions.* If you initiated the counseling meeting, it's up to you to explain your concerns to the employee. However, your job is not to point the finger or lay blame. Your employee will clam up if there's an air of criticism. The purpose of counseling is to help the person not to discipline him or her. If your employee initiated what developed into a counseling meeting, help him or her relax. Slow down what might be your normal pace. Then invite facts and opinions nonjudgmentally to draw the person out. Allow for personality differences between you. Perhaps your employee's style of expressing emotion or speaking about personal issues is very different from your own.

5. *Listen with your head and heart, then play it back.* With your head, listen to what is said. With your heart, listen to what

isn't said. Unless you have a completely open and mutually trusting relationship between you, your employee is likely to respond with a mixture of truth, tact, and fear.

Suppose you are counseling Vic about a persistent performance problem you have with him. When you ask him for input, he will certainly tell you what he believes to be true. But what if he feels his main problem is you? For example, he may feel you're a perfectionist and critical of nonessential details. Is he going to tell you this? If he fears a retaliatory result, it's not likely. And you may wonder why there's something missing in what he has told you. If he doesn't want to hurt your feelings, he may only allude to a problem with you, perhaps by saying he didn't think certain details were all that important. In either instance, you may be able to get at your real problem with Vic by playing back to him what you think he meant but didn't say. "Maybe you feel I'm concerned with pennies when I should be concerned with dollars" might be just what Vic wanted to hear. If so, then you can discuss the dollar implications of some of the details; or maybe Vic's concerns are valid and you need to back off on costly requirements for certain details.

Are you familiar with nondirective counseling? Many therapists use this technique with those they counsel. Nondirective counseling uses responses such as "You feel that . . ." "You're saying . . ." "Hmm" and silence. The idea is to draw out the respondents so they can identify and develop their own solutions to the problems they face. To counsel effectively, you don't have to become expert at nondirective counseling, but you do need to listen in an unhurried, nonjudgmental way to get at certain problems—especially personal problems that may be affecting an employee's performance. Then if you play back to the employee what you've heard, you stand a good chance of getting at the employee's real concerns.

How much should you talk during a counseling meeting? There are many variables, such as personality differences, the nature of the problem or concern, who took the initiative for the meeting, and the limitations of what can be accomplished in one meeting. But a good rule of thumb is fifty-fifty. Since you're responsible for your employee's performance, your thoughts and feelings may be just as important as those of the employee.

6. *Explore alternative solutions.* One alternative is for the employee to keep doing what he or she has been doing. Your role then is to help him or her determine the likely consequences. Often the employee has not thought this through. For example, Teri may be more concerned about justifying her actions than about how she will be affected if she doesn't learn to get along better with her work associates. You may need to help her examine whether she should address what she thinks is right or what those around her think is right.

When you and your employee are on common ground about a problem or concern, this is probably the time to ask, "What choices or alternative solutions do you feel you have?" You may have to help identify such choices or alternatives; then help your employee evaluate each. In Teri's case, possible alternatives for her might be to ask for an assignment with different work associates, to request transfer to another department, to leave the organization, or to modify her behavior. After you help her evaluate each alternative, she may decide to try to modify her behavior.

7. *Help the employee decide who will do what by when.* Counseling is not the setting to tell the employee what to do. You want him or her to make that decision so there will be commitment and follow-through. You can volunteer the actions he or she could take, but let the employee decide the course of action. In Teri's case, perhaps you can help her develop an action plan such as this:

1. Apologize today to two offended employees and ask them individually for their ideas about how she can work better with each of them.
2. Report to you by tomorrow the results of her efforts with the other two employees. Then consider any further suggestions you may have.
3. Meet with you briefly every Friday morning at eleven-thirty for four weeks to evaluate Teri's progress in modifying her behavior and in getting along.

This is a simple action plan, but it may have the potential to help Teri a lot. If it doesn't work, then further counseling may be indicated. If that doesn't work, you may have to consider disciplinary action.

8. *Follow up to ensure implementation of the planned action.* If resolution were so easy, you wouldn't have had to counsel the employee in the first place. In other words, your employee needs to know that you will continue to be involved until there is a resolution of his or her problem. Sometimes obstacles intervene, and you may be in the best position to deal with them—for example, when the employee has difficulty getting appointments.

Now let's put these counseling guidelines to work. Suppose Jennifer reports to you. Over the past couple of months, you've noticed that her output has slowed and she has developed a negative attitude. Several times you've asked her how things are going, and her response has always been "Fine." Two of her peers have made joking remarks about having to pick up the slack in her performance, but they didn't seem unduly concerned. Yesterday you mentioned the Jennifer situation to your boss, who suggested you have a counseling opportunity.

You decide to meet with Jennifer that day. You wait until she comes back from her break, and then you ask if it's a good time to see her for a half hour or so. She concurs, so you invite her into your office, which is private and quiet. You begin your meeting: "Thanks for letting me interrupt what you're doing. The reason I wanted to see you is I've noticed a decline in your output and a change in your attitude. I'm wondering if something is bothering you and if I can help." Jennifer responds by asking whether you feel she is performing satisfactorily. You explain that her performance is not your main concern but that it appears symptomatic of something that may be troubling her.

Jennifer stares back at you. Finally, she says, "I thought this was an equal opportunity organization, but I've learned otherwise." "You've learned otherwise?" you ask. Then she admits that several months earlier, she contacted human resources about a transfer to another department, where she might pursue a career more in keeping with her ambition and some outside courses she had been taking. What upset her was that an opening had occurred, and a man got the position.

You express understanding about how she feels and ask why she didn't discuss the matter with you. She answers, "I was afraid you'd react negatively about losing someone who was doing a good job and on whom you were relying." Again you express understanding and explain that your job is to help all of your staff members achieve their personal goals as a way of helping your organization achieve its goals. Jennifer looks relieved. You propose helping her explore what she might do. Together you develop alternatives:

1. Seek opportunities with another employer.
2. Contact human resources and ask why a man got the position she wanted and felt qualified for.
3. Ask human resources to arrange a meeting for her with the head of the department to which she wants to transfer, so she can find out future opportunities and required qualifications.
4. Reassess her opportunities in your department.

You discuss with her the pros and cons of each alternative, and she decides on number three. You offer to pave the way with human resources and confirm implementation of your organization's equal opportunity policy. You agree on a two-week follow-up date when you will meet again to review Jennifer's findings and perhaps to discuss replacement training.

Put yourself in Jennifer's shoes. Imagine how would you feel after this kind of counseling. Wouldn't you feel positive and motivated? That's the kind of result that effective counseling can produce.

As with some of the other supervisory skills, you don't have to be a professional to do effective counseling. If you have a mutually trusting relationship with your people, you are likely to do some good just by attempting to provide constructive help when they have problems or concerns best addressed through counseling.

The way you can hurt your department is to let crises develop with one or more individuals. This is also the way for you to have −10 performance relative to your responsibility to counsel. By contrast, the best way to help your people meet their counseling needs beyond routine requirements is to act on early-warning signs. This is also the way for you to have +10 performance relative to your responsibility to counsel—providing you invest the time and effort to do effective counseling.

Many supervisors have untapped potential to help their people through counseling. Accordingly, they also have untapped potential to improve their supervisory performance. When they realize this potential, they are more likely to be known for their *Superior Supervision.*

11

Improve

+10 PERFORMANCE: Commit to improvement goals
−10 PERFORMANCE: Defend the status quo

Are you aware that:

Your ability to create constructive change
can be the greatest single indicator of your
supervisory performance?

Recently the production vice-president of a heavy equipment manufacturer saw a need for operational improvements. He decided to make them through his supervisors, so he asked each of them to identify and commit to one improvement goal to accomplish during the subsequent three months—the first quarter of the fiscal year. Here are some of the supervisors' improvement goals:

Reduce the time taken to chase parts in the small-parts department from an estimated ten to five hours per week throughout the quarter.

Develop and install a method to reduce the time to move cars between bays from an estimated 15.0 to 7.5 hours per week throughout the quarter.

Develop and implement a written program to train new employees in the use and care of shop tools and welding equipment.

Reduce repair and rework in the finish weld-out area from an estimated 20 to 10 hours per week throughout the quarter.

Install a small-tool control program, where employees get the repaired tools they brought in or one-for-one replacements.

Develop and implement methods where engineering, loft, and layout departments will provide mutually agreeable lead times for material orders.

Develop and install a written program to ensure uniform welding procedures among 14 welders in bolsters department.
Develop and conduct a written program to train 50 plate shop
employees in how to fill out material orders correctly.
Improve the flow of materials coming from the plate shop by
rerouting destinations of parts so parts will be easier to find.
Install a quality audit system, so employees will inspect their
own parts prior to release to users.

The production vice-president was pleased with these improvement goals that his supervisors submitted to him, but he knew
that good intentions do not always produce results. Most supervisors get into routine work habits; unforeseen problems develop;
and distractions occur. But improvement requires *change.* People
tend to resist change even when it's in their best interests.

So the vice-president held a meeting with his supervisors. First,
he commended them for their improvement goals. Most of them
had good ideas, but some of them weren't planning to involve
their workers enough. The vice-president reminded them that they
were supervisors with responsibility to get results *through* their
people. Then he asked them to submit to him brief plans—one
half-page or a page—showing four to six actions each would take
to accomplish his or her goal. He said he'd like to use each plan
for individual monthly follow-up and that he was available to
help them if and when they needed him.

At the end of the quarter, the vice-president found an average
accomplishment rate of about 80 percent of the improvement
goals. In a meeting, he reported that success to the supervisors and
asked if they'd like to continue the quarterly improvement effort.
They responded favorably because they were making improvements that they and their departments actually wanted made and
benefited from. Further, there was no censure of those supervisors
whose improvement efforts were somewhat lacking.

How important are such improvement efforts? You might answer, "Not very important." Your logic might be that improvements of consequence—say, for new programs, new technology,
new equipment, or new facilities—usually involve dollar invest-
ments way beyond the approval level and control of most supervisors. For example, many organizations now have reengineering ef-

forts directed toward making dramatic process improvements of 100 percent or more to better serve customers. Or you might answer, "Very important." Your logic might be that small improvements add up to large improvements over time and that an improvement atmosphere among all employees will increase the chances for success of all improvement efforts, whether large or small. I agree with the second answer.

To illustrate how small improvements can add up, let's consider the effects of "management by 1%." Suppose you head a firm and want to improve your bottom line by making four one-percent improvements. You want to increase by one percent your sales price and your number of units sold. Also, you want to reduce by one percent your CGS (cost of goods sold) and your SG&A (sales, general, and administrative) expenses. What will be the impact on PBT (profit before tax)?

For simplicity, let's say your present sales are $10,000 from sales of 100 units at $100 apiece. Also, you have a CGS of $7,000 SG&A of $2,500 and a PBT of $500. Here's what the numbers look like after you make the four one-percent improvements:

Sales of 101 units @$101	$10,201
CGS	– 6,930
Gross Profit	$ 3,271
SG&A	– 2,475
PBT	$ 796

PBT of $796 is a bottom-line increase of 59.2 *percent* over your present PBT of $500. That's a pretty significant bottom-line impact from small improvements.

What if your improvements result in a much smaller impact than one percent? No matter. Many improvements together result in one percent or several one percents.

Most supervisors don't have to initiate or make improvements to keep their jobs. They may be encouraged to make improvements, and they may even be given credit during performance or pay reviews for the improvements they have made. But if improvements were all that important, they'd have at least one improvement goal at all times.

All supervisors need to give priority to output—production, sales, profit contribution, or the like. Usually that's short range, within a fiscal year. However, long-range output depends on improvements. Unless you improve your products, services, processes, and methods, obsolescence or replacement will result. You can either accept responsibility to make your own improvements, or you can let others make them for you. Which is in your best interest? I'd rather try to make as many improvements as I could within my own area of responsibility, wouldn't you? Further, my improvements can serve as a base for other improvements that I am asked to implement. Perhaps I can even make improvements that will be adopted by upper-level management and implemented throughout our entire organization.

Improvements are often difficult to accomplish. More positively, improvements are often a challenge—a big challenge. That's why you can distinguish yourself when you meet the challenge successfully, especially when you can do so repeatedly over a period of years. Your success at making improvements can be the best single indicator that you excel as a supervisor.

Your organization's future may well depend on the improvements you and other supervisors make on a day-to-day basis. Observe, for example, what happens to local retailers when big chains with discount purchasing and mass merchandising move into a new business community. Local retailers often have to cut back or go under because they become vulnerable to unforeseen competition.

Consider the U. S. Postal Service, which many of us thought was a virtual monopoly. Private organizations developed overnight express service, fax transmission, and electronic mail, which have had a major impact on postal revenues and operations. In manufacturing, many of us thought IBM was invulnerable. Yet emerging competition forced the firm to lose market share and, in due course, to terminate thousands of employees, a major departure from the prior policy of permanent employment.

The point is this: None of us can afford to be complacent about the security of our jobs or our organizations. That's why improvement efforts are so important. As a supervisor, you are in an excellent position to lead such efforts for your area of responsibility. And you are more likely to do so if you commit to improvement goals—which is the way to have +10 performance relative to your responsibility to improve.

There's a conceptual conviction that you and your people need to have. It is this:

The larger the pie, the more there is to divide.

In other words, the more we produce at an affordable cost, the higher our standard of living will be with a fair distribution of the proceeds.

During the Great Depression of the 1930s, someone did a cartoon that pictured a steam shovel digging a big hole for the construction of a building. Around the perimeter of the construction site were several unemployed workers with shovels. The caption read, "Why not shut down the steam shovel and put 100 workers to work?" The obvious retort was, "Why not give them teaspoons and put 10,000 workers to work?" No thinking person will buy this logic; yet many people today act as if they do. They are people:

- who hold back production or spread out their work
- who cause or tolerate significant waste
- who leave it up to others to correct or complete their work
- who promote or accept burdensome work rules that restrict output
- who seek increasingly higher levels of pay and benefits without a corresponding increase in productivity or quality
- who resist constructive change and improvement in favor of the status quo

Few supervisors are included among the first five groups above, but supervisors are well-represented in the latter group. Routinely, they defend the status quo—perhaps because of fear or insecurity or just plain stubbornness. They are the ones who have –10 performance relative to their responsibility to improve.

You can accept fully your responsibility to improve, but your efforts must be effective. One way to be effective is to adopt certain precepts.

Precepts for Making Improvements

1. You can improve every product, service, or method.
2. You and your work group have the ability to make improvements.
3. Your people will help you make improvements if they have something to gain and nothing to lose.

4. Employees need education and training about improvement whys and hows.
5. You are more likely to make improvements if you have improvement goals.
6. The easiest improvements to make are those under your control and within your present resources.
7. Team efforts can help you make interdepartmental improvements.
8. The methods you use to get acceptance for improvements are as important as the improvements themselves.
9. Your management is most likely to approve those improvements that will pay off within one year.
10. You will make meaningful improvements only if you invest scheduled time.

1. *You can improve every product, service, or method.* Nothing is forever. All needs change. Conditions change. Technologies change. Competitors change. Users change. Laws change. With change comes opportunity.

2. *You and your work group have the ability to make improvements.* All employees have creative ability, especially in the form of ideas and suggestions for improving what they do day in and day out. You can nurture and develop creativity if there is an outlet for its fruits.

3. *Your people will help you make improvements if they have something to gain and nothing to lose.* Employees resist improvements efforts if it means they lose jobs or get undesirable assignments or if they feel they've been treated unfairly as a result of past improvements. Usually, you must guarantee them—with upper management's approval—that they will get equivalent jobs if their jobs are eliminated and that normal attrition will create savings in jobs or positions. Often, better working conditions can be a significant enough gain to satisfy employees. If there is a significant dollar improvement in costs or revenues, employees along with customers, shareholders, creditors, and management usually want some financial benefit. There is an exception, and that's when an organization is fighting for survival. Then employees want job security—or at least fairness in layoffs and terminations.

4. *Employees need education and training about improvement whys and hows.* They need to know why improvements in quality

or productivity are necessary for their particular organization. This may be apparent to you but not to them. Then they need to know how you plan to make improvements. For example, they may feel you want them to work harder. One way for you to respond is a meeting with your people. Ask them to write the word *improvement* at average effort and skill for one minute. Next, ask them to do so again, but with maximum effort and with proper quality. Then ask them to calculate the difference in their production between the two exercises. Most of them will have increased production 15 to 20 percent. This is a significant improvement, but employees could not have kept up the pace of maximum effort for very long. To significantly improve the production of the word, the group should use a word processor or other technology. The implied message is: An organization's improvement potential is in improving methods much more than in having employees work harder.

5. *You are more likely to make improvements if you have improvement goals.* This is the best single way for you to excel in making improvements. You are more likely to accomplish what you target. The best place to start is on those improvements that you and your staff feel most strongly about.

6. *The easiest improvements to make are those under your control and within your present resources.* If you rely on other departments or require approvals outside your current budget, you complicate your improvement efforts. Keep it simple—at least until you and your people have realized major improvement potential within your authority and responsibility.

7. *Team efforts can help you make interdepartmental improvements.* When you do decide to tackle interdepartmental improvements, get the participation of the departments affected. If you are sales manager, for example, and want to improve your estimating software, consider using a team: one of your sales people, a software programmer, and a production engineer. Of course you will need the approval of a common superior for the three departments.

8. *The methods you use to get acceptance for improvements are as important as the improvements themselves.* Just because you build another mousetrap doesn't mean people will beat a path to your door. In other words, an improvement that is obvious to you may not be obvious to others. The reason: They see themselves affected in ways you may not appreciate. Your staff may see their

working relationships disrupted. Your management may be mostly concerned with the dollars. Those in another department may feel they're being criticized or shown up. Probably the best way to get acceptance for your improvements is to get the participation of those affected, from the outset of your improvement efforts. Then you are more likely to respond to their concerns and to gain their support.

9. *Your management is most likely to approve those improvements that will pay off within one year.* The further you project into the future, the more variables and unforeseen events there are. Management knows this from past experience and will probably react very cynically to any blue sky you project beyond known sales, costs, or budgets. Except for capital expenditures, which usually take a lot of study and justification, management's comfort level doesn't usually extend beyond one year.

10. *You will make meaningful improvements only if you invest scheduled time.* Improvements typically have little urgency. Indications of their need usually develop slowly and may not be apparent until it's too late—when, for example, your competitor offers a five-year warranty on parts and workmanship. To give your improvement efforts priority, you must invest current time and effort. One yardstick is an average of two or four hours per week throughout the year.

How many improvements can you make? Your potential is infinite. With your workers, look for:

Waste
Waiting—people standing around
Delays—materials, services, parts, equipment, orders, or
    paperwork not received on time
Errors
Rehandling
Quality defects
Missed schedules
Poor utilization of people, equipment, or facilities
Unnecessary work
Complicated methods or procedures

For those of you who like lists, the following list can give you 625 idea-starters for improvements. Listed are 25 improvement areas and 25 ways you can make improvements in each of the 25 improvement areas. For *products,* for example, consider how you can improve design, related systems, methods of use, policies for warranty, procedures for product ordering, layout for product installation, planning for product development, and so on.

List to Identify Improvement Possibilities

Improvement Area	Ways to Make Improvements
Products	Design
Services	Systems
Output	Methods
Quality	Policies
Productivity	Procedures
Revenues	Layout
Costs	Planning
Return	Scheduling
Financing	Pricing
Markets	Specifications
Customers	Standards
Prospects	Reports
Staffing	Controls
Motivation	Budgets
Cooperation	Training
Suppliers	Compensation
Materials	Incentives
Equipment	Organization
Tools	Computerization
Facilities	Automation
Conditions	Buyouts
Response	Communications
Coverage	Research
Complaints	Sampling
Compliance	Survey

Suppose a manager or supervisor in a management information systems (MIS) department wants to make improvements through the application of TQM (Total Quality Management). What improvement possibilities are there for him? One MIS manager with a large medium-size service organization recently identified his improvement possibilities by making the following comparison.

Comparison of TQM Method with Current MIS Practice

TQM Method	Our Current MIS Practice
1. Your customer defines quality	1. We define our own quality.
2. Your design dictates the product (services) you provide.	2. We let technology determine our services.
3. You build in quality rather than inspect for it.	3. We react to our quality problems or inspection findings.
4. You develop product standards and measure conformance to them.	4. We use internally focused quality standards.
5. You control only what you measure.	5. We rely more on operational performance measures than on quality or service delivery.
6. You integrate quality and productivity improvements.	6. We improve productivity more than quality.
7. You rank equally quality and financial results.	7. We promote our capability more than financial results.
8. You improve quality as a process rather than as a project.	8. We organize our efforts around projects or jobs.
9. You plan for long-term quality.	9. We concentrate on meeting current needs.
10. You commit to continuous improvement.	10. We subordinate our quality improvements to production.

To address the first item, quality definition, the MIS manager asked his internal customers (users) to rate each of their major application systems on the basis of ten criteria:

Usefulness	Responsiveness
Reliability	Flexibility
Accuracy	Efficiency
Timeliness	Ease of use
Controllability	Satisfaction

He believed this would be a major improvement toward quality definition and a step toward the application of TQM in his organization.

With potential to make many improvements, you too need to set priorities and take certain actions.

Improvement Guidelines

1. List
2. Sort
3. Target
4. Plan
5. Implement
6. Evaluate
7. Repeat

1. *List.* List all of your improvement possibilities. To involve your staff and to ensure their later support, get their ideas and suggestions—as individuals, as a group, or both. Avoid use of suggestion boxes or a suggestion system, unless you or your organization has a related program for prompt and effective administration. Otherwise, your people will suggest that you eliminate the suggestion system. Most suggestions systems become ineffective due to the time and effort they take and problems with awards.

2. *Sort.* You can classify your improvements in three ways:

those that are minor challenges—they can be accomplished in a day, week, or month

those that are major challenges—they involve other departments, require capital expenditures or unbudgeted costs, or take a year or more to accomplish

those that are moderate challenges—they are under your control, within your present resources, and can be accomplished in three to six months

Handle the first group, the *minor challenges,* as part of your day-to-day job. Perhaps all you need to do is make assignments to the authors of those improvements that appear practical and economical. Let people do their own ordering of supplies and parts, for example, or let them plan the loading of their own equipment, or let them plan and do promotions for their own customers.

Unless it's your job to plan and implement major improvements, refer the *major challenges* to those who are directly responsible. It might be the engineering department for capital expenditures, or the purchasing department to establish subcontracting relationships, or the human resources department to develop an incentive compensation program. To do benchmarking—that is, to identify and emulate the best practices in your industry—your president or chief administrator may have to take the lead to arrange mutual cooperation with competitors.

Improvements that tend to fall between the cracks are *moderate challenges*. These are the ones that have significant payout but take time and effort over a period of months to accomplish or to stay accomplished. A new procedure for waste control, for example, may be easy to install, but it is not really an improvement unless it works over a period of time.

3. *Target.* This is where you commit. I recommend setting one improvement goal of moderate challenge per quarter or six months. If necessary, break a major improvement that may take a year to accomplish into quarterly milestones or goals. I prefer a quarterly goal, so you will give priority to your improvement effort and so you can see near-term accomplishment. Select an improvement that you really want to make, but give consideration to what your staff would prefer. Caution: What your staff would prefer might be less change, even though more change may be in their best interests over time. Remember what Machiavelli once said in *The Prince:* "There is nothing more difficult to take in hand . . . than to take the lead in the introduction of a new order of things." A modern version of this is: "Change is hard."

4. *Plan.* To accomplish your improvement goal, you need a plan of major actions. The more you can rely on your people, the better. Your plan can be as simple as that of the supervisor whose quarterly goal was to reduce redos from a weekly average of twenty to five. She accomplished her goal with this plan:

1. Meet individually with key employees to:
   a. Find common causes of redos
   b. Explain department losses resulting from redos
2. Hold full department meeting on:
   a. Redos and how to combat them

     b. Department losses resulting from redos
     c. Department and employee benefits to result from achievement of the objective
  3. Make a large display chart to:
     a. Show the number of redos each day
     b. Give visible progress toward objective
  4. Make a written report of monthly progress to management.

You may also want to include in your plan dates by which each major action is to be accomplished.

5. *Implement.* Lay the groundwork for your plan within your department and with any others whose support you need. Then make assignments, and follow up to be sure improvement effort doesn't give in completely to current production. Report to your group every couple of weeks on the progress you are making and to your boss at least monthly, whether or not she requires it. A report to your boss can be a reminder to you that you can't wait until your target date to get the improvement made. Again, improvement requires change, and change is usually not easy—or else it would already have been done.

6. *Evaluate.* The supervisor above who had the goal of reducing redos projected annual savings of about $60,000 based on materials, labor-hours, and equipment-hours saved. When you report dollar results to your staff and your management, you get credibility for future improvement efforts. Ways to calculate dollar results are:

Labor or positions: Multiply the number of hours or positions by the compensation rate; then add the benefits cost, such as 25 percent.

Materials: Multiply the number of units of material by the unit value of the materials.

Equipment: Multiply the running time by the running rate; then add the cost of direct overhead—maintenance plus space—if it is not included in running rate.

Maintenance and repair: Multiply the number of maintenance hours by the maintenance rate, or the average of each repair times the number of repairs.

Interest: Multiply dollars by the interest rate for the time period.

Contingencies: Use the premium for insurance coverage such as reduction in workers' compensation costs as a result of safety improvements.

Nonmeasurable: Make a judgment about the value received. For example, the value of improved or more timely reports may be $10,000 or $20,000 if that is what your management might pay to have them for use during a twelve-month period.

7. *Repeat.* Improving cannot be a one-time project or program. It must be a continuing process for you and your organization to realize your improvement potential—or to compete successfully, or even to survive. If other members of your management do not have continuing improvement goals, you may be tempted to follow their example. I urge you to *be the example.* As a minimum, you and your department will gain.

I'm sure you get satisfaction from the routine of what you accomplish in your job. But don't you get a much greater feeling of satisfaction when you accomplish something out of the ordinary? That's what causes us to worship star performers, heroes, and heroines. You may not get that kind of recognition from your improvement efforts, but you will get additional recognition for your *Superior Supervision.*

12

Handle Pressure

+10 PERFORMANCE: Respond rationally
–10 PERFORMANCE: Respond emotionally

Are you aware that:

It isn't what happens to you—it's the way
you respond to what happens to you—that
determines whether you feel pressure?

A systems supervisor becomes *impatient* with his systems analyst who doesn't seem to understand the technical aspects of what the supervisor wants done.

A shipping supervisor loses her *temper* with a shipping clerk who missed making a critical shipment.

An engineering supervisor *compulsively* revises the design submitted to him by one of his engineers because his engineer's design was too costly to use.

An accounting supervisor *criticizes* one of her accountants because her accountant made errors in published financial reports.

A production supervisor *rejects* an employee's suggestion because it reflects on the supervisor's present method of assigning work.

A maintenance supervisor gives one of his mechanics a disproportionate number of undesirable maintenance-and-repair jobs in *retaliation* for his mechanic's blaming him for incomplete instructions on a prior overbudget repair.

A sales manager *avoids* making field trips with one of her sales representatives because she dislikes the sales representative.

A plant manager repeatedly *procrastinates* on performance evaluations with his department heads because he fears potential disagreement and dispute.

A department manager gets indigestion, becomes sullen, and loses sleep over plans for downsizing that include terminating two direct subordinates who are close friends, *internalizing* the pressure.

A purchasing manager begins to *depend* on over-the-counter and prescription tranquilizers because her purchasing agents aren't meeting construction schedules for materials and equipment.

These ten supervisors, whom you and I have seen in pressure situations, have responses that are emotional.

Emotional Responses to Pressure

- Impatience
- Temper
- Compulsion
- Criticism
- Rejection
- Retaliation
- Avoidance
- Procrastination
- Internalization
- Dependency

Are these the kinds of responses that you should have to handle pressure? No, because emotional responses are likely to hurt your ability to get results through your people.

When you face pressure situations of either short or long duration, you can respond rationally and effectively, or you can respond emotionally and ineffectively. When you respond rationally and effectively, you tend not to feel pressure because you accept what has happened. When you respond emotionally and ineffectively, you tend to feel pressure because you do not accept what has happened. Let's evaluate both responses, starting with your responsibility to handle pressure.

You may not think of handling pressure as a separate supervisory responsibility. Yet I see the ability to handle pressure as the single most distinguishing characteristic between top and bottom supervisory performance. One of the best ways to have people remember you is to display emotion. If your emotion is positive, you get a good reputation. If your emotion is negative, you get a bad reputation. More often than not, negative emotion gets associated with pressure. Your pressure is likely to be greatest when your organization is expanding or when it is constricting, as in major cost reduction efforts. However, every day you face pressures.

Pressures That Supervisors Face

- Tight deadlines
- Excessive workload
- Costly errors
- People conflicts
- Personal criticism
- Unpleasant tasks
- Change
- Career problems
- Health problems
- External concerns

• *Tight deadlines.* The people you serve, whether internal or external, have their own demands. The more they can rely on you, the easier it is on them. The problem is that too often they want their demands filled yesterday. Even when you orient them to give you adequate lead time, they make changes, and they have their own crises which they bump back to you. You and your department can either accept the fact that tight deadlines are a way of life, or you can get upset, point the finger, or respond with other negative emotions.

• *Excessive workload.* Usually, work builds up before you have all the resources you need to handle it—people, supplies, or equipment. The better job you and your people do, the better the chance that you will be asked to do more. That's nice recognition, but you will be pressured to perform at the same level that earned you the additional workload. Your workload can also be complicated by peaks of activity that may be characteristic of your business.

• *Costly errors.* As long as humans are involved, errors will occur—some of them costly. They can involve waste, lost production, lost revenues, and disrupted people relationships. How do you react when you or other people make such errors? If you've been put on the carpet for your errors, you may be tempted to put other people on the carpet when they make errors. Worse yet, you may be tempted to retaliate, internalize, or drink your lunch—all emotional responses to pressure.

• *People conflicts.* Think of everyone you have to deal with—your staff, management, peers, customers, suppliers, union officials, and others. Conflicts are inevitable—disagreements, disputes, distrust, dislikes. Your more critical relationships are with those people with whom you deal the most. How well do you get along with each of your people? How well do you get along with your boss? If, for example, your department fears you, your work environment is likely to be tense. Tension will also result if you fear your boss—perhaps because you were brought up to fear anyone in authority. Your mind and body will register tension and can magnify your emotional response to conflicts or other pressures. On the other hand, if your boss and your staff see you as a piece of cake, it may be because you fear confrontation and do everything you can to avoid it, including avoidance and procrastination—both emotional responses to pressure. I'm reminded of the comic who said, "I love humanity. It's people I can't stand."

• *Personal criticism.* The more conscientious you are, the more likely you are to try to avoid criticism. So when you are criticized, you may respond more emotionally than others—for example, by criticizing back. If your boss is the one who's criticizing you, you may respond with greater and greater resolve to avoid future criticism. So you yield to a compulsion to work longer and harder, and you get a reputation as a workaholic. One likely result is, you do the work that your staff is qualified to do, and they learn to rely more and more on you. Your situation is complicated if you have a detail-oriented boss who criticizes you when you don't know all the details of your operation.

• *Unpleasant tasks.* How do you respond when you have to:

Discipline one of your workers?
Terminate an employee?
Give bad news to your boss?
Give bad news to your department?
Give performance evaluations?
Develop and get approval for budgets and other plans?
Prepare written reports for management?
Make a presentation to your peers or to upper-level management?

These are examples of tasks that every supervisor has and that many supervisors consider unpleasant. Depending on how unpleasant you find such tasks, you may feel pressure and respond emotionally in one or more ways.

• *Change.* Every supervisor faces change—whether in the form of new needs that have to be met, new problems that have to be solved, or improvements that have to be dealt with. It's easier to accept change that others have to make than change that you and your work group have to make. Many people associate fear with change, and if you're as human as others, you may have similar fear. The question is: In your role as a supervisor, to what extent do you react emotionally to change? If your tendency is to reject employee suggestions, for example, you may be reacting more emotionally than you realize.

• *Career problems.* To what extent have you had these occurrences?

> You did not receive the pay raise or bonus you expected.
> A less-deserving peer got a higher pay raise or bonus than you.
> You did not get the assignment or promotion you expected.
> A peer whom you felt was less qualified got the assignment or promotion you expected.

Whether or not these have been your past experiences, to what extent do you have these feelings now?

> Your boss gives preferential treatment to one or more of your peers.
> Your boss doesn't care for you personally.
> Your boss takes most or all of the credit for your accomplishment.
> Your staff, your peers, or others have hurt your reputation—perhaps even through back-stabbing.
> You are a victim of internal politics played better by others.
> You feel dead-ended, either because of your job or the plight of your organization.

I find that most supervisors like their jobs and feel they are being treated fairly. But I also find a fair number of exceptions. If you are one of those exceptions, you may feel an underlying day-to-day grinding pressure that affects your attitude, your supervisory performance, and your career progress.

• *Health problems.* Just like everyone else, supervisors get health problems—whether physical or mental. Because they have leadership roles, however, sometimes they do not want to admit to themselves or others that they are feeling the pressure of health concerns—unattended symptoms, lack of energy, concentration difficulty, worry, or even depression. Sometimes the problem goes away. Other times it doesn't without professional help.

I recall my own experience a few years ago when I began to get some scary panic attacks. They came out of nowhere, for no particular reason. Because I couldn't pinpoint the cause, I delayed taking any action, hoping they would go away. They didn't. I began to fear making people contacts, which are essential to my work. Finally I went to see my doctor. He gave me an exam and did tests. Then he recommended a psychologist, who helped me recognize symptoms I didn't even know I had—tight stomach, tight neck and shoulder muscles, and teeth grinding. In due course, we figured out the culprit—overcommitment, too many things to do, too many promises, and an inability to do it all. I slowed up, got deadlines extended, canceled noncritical commitments, and avoided most additional burdens. Almost immediately, the panic attacks went away. Gradually I regained my confidence in making people contacts, and I got back to normal. My only regret was that I hadn't acted earlier on my symptoms.

Supervisors who respond emotionally to growing or recurring health problems—in my case, through avoidance and procrastination—hurt not only themselves but their people. They're kidding themselves if they think their people don't notice or aren't affected.

• *External concerns.* Many people have domestic, financial, legal, or other concerns outside of work. As a supervisor, however, the way you respond to such concerns can affect your performance, which in turn can affect the performance of your people. If your concerns persist and remain unresolved, then pressure can build up within you.

Emotional responses to the pressures you face will generally be ineffective. When you curse, blame, deny, point, fight, delay or hide, you have −10 performance relative to your responsibility to handle pressure.

When you respond rationally to the pressures you face, you will generally be effective. What are ways to respond rationally?

Rational Responses to Pressure

- Questioning
- Listening
- Objectivity
- Calmness
- Correction
- Care
- Problem-solving
- Reliance
- Timeliness
- Prevention

I began this chapter with ten examples of supervisors who responded emotionally to the pressures they faced. How might each supervisor have responded rationally?

Our systems supervisor might have asked his systems analyst an occasional *question* to validate progressive understanding of instructions before working up a lather of *impatience*.

Our shipping supervisor might have *listened* objectively and calmly to her shipping clerk about what happened to the critical shipment before jumping to emotional conclusions and losing her *temper*. Then together they might have taken corrective action. Perhaps they could have air-expressed a partial shipment, gotten a reprieve from the customer, or proposed a substitute product.

Our *compulsive* engineering supervisor might have apologized to his engineer for not clarifying the cost considerations. Then he might have relied on his engineer to make a revised, *objective* design—perhaps with a little coaching from a cohort.

Our *critical* accounting supervisor might have *calmly* asked her accountant to help her assess and compensate for any damage done from errors in the financial reports. Then perhaps they could have determined how to prevent future errors.

Our production supervisor who *rejected* the employee's suggestion might have listened objectively, asked questions to ensure mutual understanding, and helped develop a *corrected* or replacement suggestion.

Our maintenance supervisor, instead of *retaliating,* might have listened calmly and *carefully* to his mechanic's blame, asked questions to see how the mechanic would have avoided going over budget on the repair, and developed together future preventive action. (Note: If the maintenance supervisor retaliates against the mechanic, additional problems will surely result.)

Our sales manager might have taken a *problem-solving* approach to evaluate what is likely to happen if she continues to *avoid* going out with her sales representative. Perhaps her boss will hold her accountable, or the sales representative will quit, or she will lose support from her other people.

Our plant manager, instead of *procrastinating,* might have *relied* on his boss or someone in human resources for guidance about how to handle potential disagreement and dispute during performance evaluations.

Our department manager, instead of *internalizing,* might have relied on professional counsel for *timely* guidance, as soon as physical and mental symptoms developed. Perhaps he has health problems unrelated to the termination of his friends.

Our purchasing manager might have relied on her boss, her staff, and the construction manager to help her solve current problems and *prevent* future problems. Perhaps construction schedules can be adjusted or substitute materials could be used or visits to vendors can result in better service. If her *dependency* on tranquilizers became deep-seated, she should certainly get professional help.

Now you may wonder, "How can any supervisor always respond rationally to pressure?" The answer is that no one can, but some supervisors do much better than others. Those who accept whatever happens and respond rationally are those who are likely to have +10 performance relative to their responsibility to handle pressure. Does this describe you?

Your reputation for handling pressure may be better than you think, or it may be weaker than you suspect. Either way, you could probably improve your reaction to pressure.

Guidelines for Handling Pressure

1. Evaluate how well you handle pressure now—including your impact on people.
2. Identify foreseeable pressure situations to which you need to respond better.
3. Develop conditioned responses.
4. Get professional help if needed.
5. Do preventive planning.
6. Check your progress.

1. *Evaluate how well you handle pressure now—including your impact on people.* To what extent do you become impatient, lose your temper, give in to a compulsion to do something not in your best interests, criticize your people or others, reject ideas and suggestions, take retaliatory action against those you feel have done you in, avoid people relationships or other concerns, procrastinate about unpleasant tasks, internalize the pressures you feel, or yield to dependency behavior? If you do so rarely, you probably don't have a problem. If you do so sometimes, you may have a problem. If you do so often, you have a problem about how to handle one or more pressures. If you're not sure, get an evaluation from someone you trust to be open with you and who is in a position to know. It might be your boss, one of your staff, a peer, or someone else at work. I don't advise your using your mate or significant other because of the complications of your personal relationship.

2. *Identify foreseeable pressure situations to which you need to respond better.* If certain pressure situations have been a problem for you in the past, they are likely to be so in the future. So, for example, if you're in the habit of working sixty to seventy hours a week, you are likely to continue doing so, whether or not your workload demands it. It becomes a compulsion that can result in your getting a reputation for poor work organization, poor delegation, or poor staffing. Your staff, your management, and others are not likely to credit you for the ambition, example-setting, devotion, and loyalty you may feel. Further, your mate, children, significant other, relatives, or friends are likely to see themselves as victims and will find other ways to meet their needs for sharing, companionship, and parenting.

3. *Develop conditioned responses.* If you feel a need for improvement, chances are you have a pressing need to improve your response to the pressures you face. Then you have the challenge of overcoming a behavior pattern or habit. The key is to develop a conditioned response—decide in advance how you will respond to those pressure situations you are likely to face, and condition yourself to respond that way.

Conditioned Responses to Pressure Situations

Pressure Situation	Conditioned Response
Tight deadline	*Stay cool*—seek compromise, revise priorities, create new resources
Excessive workload	*Think dollars*—limit your time to where the big dollars are; delegate
Costly errors	*Accept blame*—maintain cooperative attitudes to correct and prevent
People conflicts	*Reverse roles*—put yourself in the other person's shoes
Personal criticism	*Invite suggestions*—throw your critic off guard
Unpleasant tasks	*Evaluate consequences*—determine how you and others will be affected by delay or avoidance
Change	*Respond positively*—ask questions and listen before deciding
Career problems	*Get counsel*—accept responsibility for where you are; seek guidance from boss or others
Health problems	*Validate symptoms*—yield to health suspicions; see a doctor
External concerns	*Get help*—rely on professionals when your work is affected

Note how short each conditioned response is. That's to make them easier to remember. Repeat the response that applies to you so your memory bank will record the message and play it back to you over your prior emotional response. One idea: Put up a small sign with your response on it so you can see it repeatedly during your workday. Then try out your conditioned response. Chances are you will feel better than with your prior emotional response, but it may take time for people to believe you've changed and for your emotions to adjust. You must believe you *can* improve. Remember what psychologist William James observed; "The greatest discovery of my generation is that human beings can alter their lives by altering their attitudes of mind."

4. *Get professional help if needed.* If you're not getting relief from the pressures you face, you have two choices: You can continue doing what you're doing, or you can seek help. Your best source of help is likely to be a professional. You will resist such help if you feel it's a sign of weakness to have to get outside input. But aren't you likely to get the best solutions when you combine input from both the inside and the outside? If you wait until a crisis develops, you may have no choice other than to rely on a professional. That professional may come from another part of your organization or from the outside.

5. *Do preventive planning.* You can predict most pressure situations merely by looking at what has happened in the past. That's why preventive maintenance exists, for example. You do scheduled maintenance and repair currently to prevent costly breakdowns and crises from occurring in the future. I'm sure you do preventive planning now, but can you do more to prevent or handle more effectively tight deadlines, excessive workloads, costly errors, people conflicts, and change?

6. *Check your progress.* The best way for you to be sure you've improved in the way you handle certain pressure situations is to get periodic input from those who know. The best sources will be your workers, boss, or peers. Don't make a project out of it, but you can solicit informal comments. Questions you might ask are: "Do you think things are going more smoothly now?" or "How's employee morale now?" or "What's our progress in dividing the workload?"

You are more likely to have –10 performance when you respond emotionally to pressure. By the same token, you are more likely to have +10 performance when you respond rationally to pressure.

Two supervisors in separate organizations stand out in my mind for +10 performance. Both had the opportunity to make a presentation in meetings of their top management. They used preparation to overcome their public speaking fears, and they both did so well each of them got double promotions within a couple of months. Their promotions were largely the result of the impressions they created during their thirty-minute presentations.

I wish I could promise similar results for you when you excel at handling pressure. But I believe I can promise that the more effectively you respond to the pressures you face, the less pressure you will feel to meet all the requirements for *Superior Supervision.*

13

Control

+10 PERFORMANCE: Control your own performance
−10 PERFORMANCE: Let others control your performance

Are you aware that:

Any strong tendency you have to blame
others for your performance problems can
impede your career progress more than
any other single factor?

D ave Rath is maintenance supervisor for a nonprofit organization that provides housing services to university students. He
has a staff of mechanics, carpenters, and painters for maintenance, repair, and renovation of more than a thousand apartments
and rooms. One day his boss, the operations manager, came to
him with this question; "How do you know if you're monitoring
all the critical areas for control of the maintenance function?"
"Good question," Dave responded. "Let me give it some thought
and get back to you."

No one had ever asked Dave that question before. He felt he
had been doing a good job. He had an annual plan that he was implementing; he kept good records; and he made whatever reports
were required of him. But now he began to wonder if he was missing something.

Dave decided to consult four of his key people. Together, they
agreed to start from scratch—by assuming they had no controls.
They asked themselves, "What do we need to control to ensure
our short- and long-range effectiveness?" After a couple of meetings, they developed the following list:

Controls for financial results
- Dollars of contribution toward corporate overhead (rental revenue less controllable maintenance costs)
- Dollars of overtime incurred

Controls for operational results
- Timeliness of maintenance service to student renters
- Work order completion progress
- Quality of renovation
- Number of maintenance requests received (effectiveness indicator for preventive maintenance)
- Quantity and quality of preventive maintenance
- Utilities performance level—quantity and quality
- Emergency readiness (disruption of utilities service, student crisis, other)
- Safety readiness
- Turnover of craftspeople
- Government inspection readiness
- Value received from suppliers
- Economical balance between providing in-house service and buy-out service
- Ambiance of apartments and rooms for students

Controls for prevention and handling of disasters
- Large dollar overruns on contracts
- Unforeseen major capital expenditures (such as reroofing, rewiring, or repiping)
- Major failure of utilities
- Loss of key people
- Major accident
- Act of God

Dave already had control reports for many of the items on this list. For example, he had a monthly report showing progress toward an annual objective for dollar contribution to corporate overhead (often called profit contribution in for-profit firms). This report reflected Dave's budget compliance and the impact of maintenance on rental revenue. He also had a weekly overtime report and a daily report showing the percentage of maintenance requests that were responded to within twenty-four hours. He considered the latter report to be his key indicator of day-to-day performance.

What he discovered, however, was that he was not monitoring all of his critical control areas, such as government inspection readiness, value received from suppliers, economical balance between providing in-house service and buy-out service, and the whole area of disaster control. He concluded he needed planned monitoring in these areas at least a couple of times per year.

Dave reviewed with his boss the results of his controls review. His boss reacted favorably but wanted more emphasis on preventive maintenance. Dave was pleased with his boss's response, but he was even more pleased with the feeling that he was more in control of his job than he had ever been.

Have you ever done the kind of control review that Dave did? Most supervisors have not. Their tendency is to rely on others for the kinds of controls they should have. When they do, they make control errors.

Control Errors That Supervisors Make

- They report only what they're asked to report.
- They wait for control data.
- They rely on their boss.
- They point the finger.

• *They report only what they're asked to report.* Every supervisor must comply with existing control systems to report output, sales, quality, performance against budget, and the like. Such reporting provides supervisors with helpful control data, but it is not tailored to all of the control needs for individual supervisors. So when supervisors rely only on reports required by others, they have incomplete control data. In part, they have abrogated their responsibility to control.

• *They wait for control data.* Here it is the third week of the month, and the supervisor says, "I don't know how we did last month. We haven't gotten our monthly figures yet." My reaction is, "So what? If you can't get others to provide you with the control data you need, *get your own data* in time to take appropriate control action for *this month's results*!" One way for supervisors to get their own control data is to use existing data coupled with estimates. Who cares whether their sales or revenue or cost or budget figures are accurate down to a gnat's eyebrow? Such accuracy is unnecessary for control purposes. Accountants usually feel they need to be accurate, so often they wait until all of the billing is done or until all of the suppliers' invoices are in. Then the report from accounting will be accurate, but it will be late for control purposes.

• *They rely on their boss.* Many supervisors stick to the routine of their jobs and hope for the best. They leave it to their boss to tell them to hold prices or change the sales direction or reduce costs or increase on-time deliveries or install quality controls or get new software or revise the layout or improve staffing or solve interdepartmental bottlenecks. These are the kinds of major control actions that the boss initiates when supervisors do not accept full responsibility for doing whatever is necessary to achieve or exceed objectives. Such supervisors are particularly prone to sit on their hands when their organizations are having performance problems. They often feel insecure and don't want to rock the boat.

• *They point the finger.* When they are not achieving their objectives, many supervisors make comments such as these:

> "I told my staff what I expected."
> "I don't have the right people."
> "We need better equipment."
> "We're bound by our work rules."
> "Our suppliers were late."
> "Our prices are too high."
> "My budget limits what I can do."
> "Our computer hamstrings us."
> "We can't do our job if other parts of our organization don't do theirs."
> "Our customers expect too much."

This is the most serious of all control errors—the tendency to point the finger at employees, bosses, peers, customers, clients, users, suppliers, unions, competitors, and government. What happens when you point the finger? You're acknowledging that you're not in control—that you're somewhat of a victim—that other people control your performance. "But aren't these beyond my control?" you may respond. The answer is: Only if you think so.

If you believe you have factors you can't control, such as customer emergencies, supplier glitches, or inadequate resources, then you do. On the other hand, if you believe everything is controllable, you can foresee and handle customer emergencies—you can foresee and handle supplier glitches—and you can foresee and handle any problems caused by inadequate resources.

Take inadequate resources, for example. Maybe you can use direct mail to get customers to come to you rather than your going to them—or do outsourcing for computer services rather than buy computer hardware—or do subcontracting—or make exchange arrangements with competitors—or get volunteer effort—or get concessions from users—or delay a program—or modify objectives. There's always something you can do.

If you run out of ideas, do some research. Contact your workers, your boss, your peers, your counterparts in other organizations, and your professionals inside and outside your organization. Or read some articles and books. Or get some training, from conferences, meetings, seminars, courses. Whatever you do, accept responsibility for the results you get, good or bad, and resolve to control all major factors that affect your performance. You may not be able to foresee all eventualities, such as acts of God, but your attitude must be that you can—for example, through insurance. When you control your own performance, you have +10 performance relative to your responsibility to control. The way to have −10 performance is to point the finger, which in effect lets others control your performance.

How can you avoid control errors and have a +10 performance?

Control Guidelines

1. Install an indicator of performance for each of your critical areas of performance.
2. Install one key indicator of day-to-day performance.
3. Get control data in time to take appropriate control action.
4. Rely on your people to control their performance.
5. Watch dollars, not pennies.
6. Monitor results before methods.
7. Use graphics to show performance.
8. Make an annual report of accomplishment.

1. *Install an indicator of performance for each of your critical areas of performance.* Do as Dave Rath did. Meet with your key employees to determine what you need to control to ensure your short- and long-range effectiveness. Consider output, quality, rev-

enues, costs, staffing, motivation, training, methods, disaster control, and improvements. Next, decide what needs to be measured at what frequency to get your performance indicators. No doubt you already make and get reports for many of the performance indicators covering areas such as output, quality, revenues, and cost control. But like Dave Rath, you need to determine whether you have all the performance indicators you need to excel over both the short range (days, weeks, months) and long range (one to five years).

2. *Install one key indicator of day-to-day performance.* I like to distinguish between financial and operating controls. Financial controls help you achieve financial results relating to revenue, profit contribution production, shipments, inventory, costs, and the like. Usually you accomplish financial results over weeks, months, or a year. Operating controls help you achieve your financial results, but they do so on a day-to-day basis generally before financial data is available. Your most important operating control is your key indicator of day-to-day performance. In Dave Rath's case, he used percentage of maintenance requests responded to within twenty-four hours as his key indicator. Other examples of key indicators are:

Performance Area	Key Indicator of Day-to-Day Performance
Sales	Number of sales calls made on target accounts
Production	Percentage of on-time deliveries
Engineering	Design-hours of backlog
Computer Services	Percentage of computer uptime-hours compared to demand

A key indicator of day-to-day performance is like an early-warning system. You get advance notice about whether you need to take control action to achieve your planned results.

3. *Get control data in time to take appropriate control action.* Some supervisors confuse measurement or reporting with control. Control means action. Getting or making a report gives you control data, but in itself it is not control. You get control only when you take action to achieve or enhance results. I'm not suggesting you need to take control action every time you get control data,

but you must certainly do so at times. Otherwise, you don't need the control data.

This raises the question: How often do you need control data? The answer is: The closer you are to where the work is done, the more frequently you need control data. If you are a first-line supervisor, you probably need control data daily. If you are a second-line supervisor, you probably need control data weekly. If you have higher-level supervisory responsibility, you probably need control data monthly, as you should be able to rely on your direct reports to take weekly or daily control action. Control action results when you help eliminate bottlenecks, resolve interdepartmental performance problems, instruct or coach individuals, and take other appropriate actions consistent with your responsibility as a supervisor.

We've been discussing control data of an objective type, but what about subjective control data? You get subjective control data when you spend time with your people individually and together. You might call this "supervising by getting around." If you are people-oriented, you may feel that subjective control data is most important. If you are technically oriented, you may feel that objective control data with measurable performance indicators is most important. Check with your employees and your boss. They can help you determine the right balance.

4. *Rely on your people to control their performance.* If you have strong temperamental tendencies to control, you may find it difficult to delegate and rely on people. Yet you must do so if you want to tap the potential of your staff and if you want to free yourself for additional responsibility. Your department has the ability to monitor and control its own performance, providing you give it the tools. They need the same perspective and control data that you have, so you must give them training and information. Too often supervisors get the control data before their staff does; then supervisors use the control data as a weapon to beat up their staff when performance is lacking.

If your employees get prompt control data relative to their output, schedules, cost control, and the like, they can usually determine and take their own control action just as readily as you. But you must take clear to them why it is in their own best interest to do so, what they need to do, and when they can get your help. By relying on your staff in this way, you can implement "management by exception." This means you spend your time where significant problems and opportunities are. There's no reason to give each member of your department equal attention and time if their needs differ and you can achieve better overall results. You still have the same responsibility to control when you rely on your staff, but you make it easier on yourself and you empower employees to perform with less supervision.

5. *Watch dollars, not pennies.* The place for you to achieve big-dollar results is where the big dollars are. If you concentrate on saving pennies—on the assumption that the dollars will take care of themselves—you orient your workers to watch pennies more than dollars, too. One supervisor monitored office supplies down to pads of paper. Yet his department had billing errors that amounted to thousands of dollars. Another supervisor monitored the expense reports of the salespeople down to maid tips. Yet the sales representatives wasted thousands of dollars in travel due to the way accounts were assigned. Another supervisor got the last drop of blood from suppliers but got inferior customer service, which increased production costs by many thousands of dollars. Supervisors who pinch pennies usually irritate their staff. Any savings that result are offset many times by negative impact on employee morale and productivity.

6. *Monitor results before methods.* No doubt you achieved your present level of responsibility because you performed well. It's only natural that you want your staff to emulate you. The result may be that you evaluate your people more by how they perform than by what they achieve. If they are achieving planned results, why should Daryl sell like you, or Irma design like you, or Manny program like you, or Betti do setup like you? On the other hand, if they're not performing, you must evaluate their methods; if necessary, you can even impose on them some of the methods that worked for you. Of course, you have the right to expect compliance with any critical procedure such as order entry or cash control.

7. *Use graphics to show performance.* Most people understand pictures better than numbers. So you can make your control data more meaningful to your staff if you present it graphically. Take quality, for example. A production supervisor for a sporting goods manufacturer used weekly charts to help reduce rework and scrap, like the one in the chart shown.

Weekly charts such as this one dramatize quality problems in a way that gets everyone's attention. With today's computer software programs, such charts are easy to prepare.

You can also use charts to show trends, such as causes of quality problems. For example, the 40-30-30 rule states that manufacturing errors and waste are typically caused 40 percent by design, 30 percent by the production process, and 30 percent by suppliers. You can remedy such causes with the help of charts that show monthly over a period of a year or two what is happening. Often

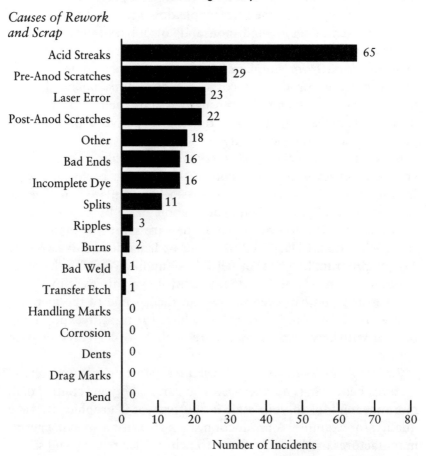

NUMBER OF REWORK AND SCRAP INCIDENTS AT LASER
FOR TENT TUBES, METERS, X-BOW BOLTS
Week Ending January 12

Causes of Rework and Scrap

Cause	Number of Incidents
Acid Streaks	65
Pre-Anod Scratches	29
Laser Error	23
Post-Anod Scratches	22
Other	18
Bad Ends	16
Incomplete Dye	16
Splits	11
Ripples	3
Burns	2
Bad Weld	1
Transfer Etch	1
Handling Marks	0
Corrosion	0
Dents	0
Drag Marks	0
Bend	0

Number of Incidents

changes occur so gradually that you may not notice a trend until it bites you in the posterior.

8. *Make an annual report of accomplishment.* Very few supervisors do this, but it is an excellent way for you to:

- Evaluate your own performance for the past year
- Communicate to your management your contribution to the success of your organization
- Plan for next year

In effect, this is an annual control report that you submit to your boss. What should the format be for such a report? Here is one example.

Controller's Annual Report of Accomplishment

TO: President
FROM: Controller
SUBJECT: Annual report of accomplishment as related to action plan

PRIMARY PRIORITY

1. Improved completeness and accuracy of monthly reporting to show performance against budget.
2. Reviewed/strengthened internal control procedures for more complete/accurate accounting of revenue, expenses, assets, and liabilities.
3. Advanced annual budget preparation by three months to allow greater participation by tenants council and finance committee of board.
4. Developed/implemented method to determine when and how revenue will be recognized for accounting/tax purposes.
5. Developed/implemented policy to optimize return on temporary cash operating reserve.
6. Initiated and proposed financing solution (through alternative funding and debt retirement) for housing contract.
7. Identified tax factors that can affect property tax exemption and non-profit status company over both short and long term.

8. Developed/implemented program to make more efficient and less costly use of computer equipment.
9. Reorganized/staffed/trained for three changes in accounting department.
10. Administered annual audit process that resulted in unqualified opinion from outside CPA firm.

SECONDARY PRIORITY

1. Developed/got approval of program for use/management of computer network system and related software.
2. Streamlined payroll system and freed accounting time with new outside service.
3. Updated/redesigned chart of accounts to be more accurate and user-friendly.
4. Developed working relationships with two local banks.
5. Evaluated and participated in selection of new property management software.
6. Established effective working relationship with outside CPA firm.

This report shows the accomplishments of a controller with a staff of only a few people. Note the report is only one page of one-sentence accomplishments classified by primary and secondary priority. It's the kind of report that puts an annual cap on what you and your people have done and it helps you distinguish yourself as a supervisor.

By following the above guidelines, you take control of your own destiny. You avoid letting others control your performance because you control your own performance.

One way to describe the supervisor's job is this:

- Decide what to do;
- Do it;
- See that you did it.

Control is seeing that you did it—through your people, of course. It's the third major responsibility you have to show that you can excel through *Superior Supervision*.

14

Application on the Job

Are you aware that:

The likelihood of your implementing *Superior Supervision* beyond your present skill level is low unless you get an emotional jolt to do so?

Technology has created what many now call the Information Age. The result is, you and I get bombarded with information—both at work and away from work. Our challenge is what to do about the information. We can let it pass by, or we can act on it, physically, mentally, nutritionally, medically, socially, politically, philosophically, religiously, environmentally, economically, recreationally, domestically, educationally, vocationally, or professionally. So when you or I read a skill-improvement book, what do we do about it? We're probably fortunate if we apply one or two ideas.

I'd be satisfied if you applied only one or two good ideas from *Superior Supervision,* but I'd to see you get more value from it than that. That's not likely, however, unless you have a good reason to do so. Good intentions won't do it. If you are like most people, you need an emotional jolt to cause you to spring into action.

Many supervisors do their jobs under the assumption that they're functioning effectively in all major areas of their responsibility. But others with whom they work have a different perspective. Take Ben, Mike, Gina, and Chris.

• *Ben* is a production supervisor. He feels he is doing a good job and he is well accepted by everyone. He came up through the ranks, has learned every job, and prides himself on being able to solve any problems his people have. He believes in setting the example and in asking his people to do only what he himself is willing to do. His people come to him regularly for help and decisions. Every day he feels productive and needed.

• *Mike* is an office supervisor. He became a supervisor because he excelled in several capacities as an individual performer. He gets results, but he has an autocratic style that comes across as "Do it because I say so!" Some of his people respond cooperatively. Others feel some resentment and drag their feet when responding. He knows he has credibility and can't understand why certain of his people don't want to do things right.

• *Gina* is a sales manager. Before getting into management, she had an outstanding sales record. Along with the other salespeople, she was on straight commission and liked being paid directly in relation to the results she achieved. She believes that's the way all good salespeople are motivated. Yet some of her more experienced salespeople don't achieve the sales levels she knows they are capable of achieving. When they get to a certain earnings level, they seem to slack off and coast.

• *Chris* is a client services supervisor. She has responsibility for order entry, order scheduling, order expediting, client inquiries, and claims and complaints. Her firm has expanded and has introduced some new services that have caused complications in client service. Her people have suggested changes in certain procedures, but she believes adherence to present procedures is best because they have been more than adequate in the past.

Ben is not realizing his potential to delegate. Mike is not realizing his potential to get cooperation. Gina is not realizing her potential to motivate. And Chris is not realizing her potential to make procedural improvements. They also appear to lack awareness of their performance deficiencies.

In my consulting, I find it commonplace for supervisors to rate their own performance higher than the rating their staff members, peers, and bosses give them. When they are told about the disparities, they are usually surprised and want to improve their supervisory performance.

My question to you is: Do you need to improve your supervisory performance? You may not know until something happens that reflects on your supervisory performance or until you act to find out whether you need to improve your supervisory performance. Several things can happen to reflect on your supervisory performance.

What Can Happen to Reflect on Your Supervisory Performance

- You lose key people.
- Complaints or grievances are filed against you.
- You get a disappointing performance review.
- Your raise or bonus is less than you expected.
- Someone else gets the promotion you wanted.

• *You lose key people.* One indication that you are an effective supervisor is that your staff will follow you anywhere. If you get transferred or promoted, for example, they will seek to come to work for you in your new capacity. By contrast, if people, especially your key employees, are quitting or transferring, you may not be functioning effectively as a supervisor. You may be the cause of their moving on. If you come to realize this, you get the impetus—an emotional jolt—to improve your ways.

• *Complaints or grievances are filed against you.* If this has ever happened to you, you probably suffered—whether or not the action against you was justified. It's something like automobile insurance. If you have an accident, it goes against your record, whether or not you were at fault. After two or three accidents, your insurance carrier may drop you. With employee complaints or grievances, you run the risk that your management may come to view you similarly. So if you accept what has happened, you are shocked into constructive action. You get an emotional jolt to review and possibly improve your supervisory performance.

• *You get a disappointing performance review.* Whether or not your organization has a formal performance review process, your boss is likely to express himself or herself about your performance. Your review can even be nonverbal if your boss begins to give you the cold shoulder or excludes you from activities in which you used to participate. You can either point the finger at your boss, or you can use your performance review as a stimulus—an emotional jolt—for improving your supervisory performance.

• *Your raise or bonus is less than you expected.* I know a supervisor to whom this happened three times in a row. After the first two times, she rejected the idea that there was anything materially wrong with her performance in spite of her boss's best efforts to communicate her improvement needs. After the third time, she finally got the message. She saw that her job was on the line, so she got an emotional jolt to improve her people relationships which in due course was recognized in her pay.

• *Someone else gets the promotion you wanted.* You can blame the politics on your organization and feel victimized, or you can react constructively. When you react constructively, you use the other candidate's promotion as the motivation—an emotional jolt—to see what you need to do to improve.

Successful people in all endeavors often have this philosophy: If you get a lemon, make lemonade. That's what you can do when something happens that may reflect on your supervisory performance. Alternatively, you can take one or more preventive actions.

Preventive Actions You Can Take to Find Out Whether You Need to Improve Your Supervisory Performance

1. Initiate evaluations of your performance.
2. Solicit informal suggestions for your improvement.
3. Conduct an internal customer survey.
4. Seek regular guidance from a career sponsor.
5. Implement a continuing program for self-development.

1. *Initiate evaluations of your performance.* Not everyone believes in performance evaluations. I'm sympathetic with this view when those affected lack confidence in the way the evaluations are done or used. On the other hand, evaluations can be used effectively to let willing participants know where they stand and to give them a basis for further self-development.

To realize your supervisory potential, you need to find out where you need to improve. One way is to initiate your own performance evaluations. If you want ratings of your performance in each of the twelve areas of supervisory responsibility covered in this book, you may find the "Supervisory Performance Evaluation" form helpful.

Your advantage to using this form is that you control who sees it and how it's used. You might ask your boss to complete it, or

SUPERVISORY PERFORMANCE EVALUATION

Name of Supervisor Being Rated	Optional: Name of Rater	Date of Rating

Purpose: Provides supervisor with basis for reinforcing and improving his or her current supervisory performance.

Rating scale:
EXCELLENT — Excels, but is not perfect
GOOD — Meets requirements of position
FAIR — Gets by, but is deficient
POOR — Unsatisfactory performance

Optional: Add plus or minus to each rating.

RESPONSIBILITY	PERFORMANCE RATING	COMMENT (Explanation or Suggestion)
1. **Plans:** Determines what needs to be done by whom by when at what cost for a planning period such as a month, quarter, or year.		
2. **Delegates:** Assigns work, responsibility, and authority so his or her people can make maximum use of their abilities.		
3. **Gives Instructions:** Gives day-to-day assignments to his or her people so they do what needs to be done when it should be done in the manner he or she wants it done.		
4. **Gets Cooperation:** Helps his or her people work willingly and effectively as individuals and groups.		

RESPONSIBILITY	PERFORMANCE RATING	COMMENT (Explanation or Suggestion)
5. **Solves Problems:** Develops and implements solutions to day-to-day supervisory problems.		
6. **Staffs:** Sees that a qualified person is selected for each of his or her positions.		
7. **Trains:** Teaches individuals and groups how to do their jobs.		
8. **Motivates:** Determines and helps his or her people meet their personal needs for tangible and intangible compensation over both short and long range.		
9. **Counsels:** Holds a private discussion with an individual about how he or she might do better work, solve a personal problem, or realize ambition.		
10. **Improves:** Develops better methods and procedures to ensure quality and to increase productivity.		

RESPONSIBILITY	PERFORMANCE RATING	COMMENT (Explanation or Suggestion)
11. **Handles Pressure:** Fulfills responsibility in the face of emotional stress or pressing demands.		
12. **Controls:** Measures progress and takes corrective action when needed to achieve his or her objectives.		

OVERALL PERFORMANCE RATING & MOST IMPORTANT
SUGGESTION FOR IMPROVEMENT

you might try it out on one or two of your staff members who you believe will give you constructive input about your performance. Also, ask the evaluators to record any comments about each rating—particularly if a rating is below average. At the bottom of the form, ask the evaluators to give you a rating of your overall supervisory performance, plus the most important skill for you to address. Your evaluators may be hesitant to write their comments, but encourage them to do so. You will probably find those observations give you the most information about what you do well and what you could do better. A completed sample of the form is shown.

SUPERVISORY PERFORMANCE EVALUATION

Name of Supervisor Being Rated	Optional: Name of Rater	Date of Rating
Les Braxton	*C.F.*	*2/20*

Purpose: Provides supervisor with basis for reinforcing and improving his or her current supervisory performance.

Rating scale:

EXCELLENT	Excels, but is not perfect
GOOD	Meets requirements of position
FAIR	Gets by, but is deficient
POOR	Unsatisfactory performance

Optional: Add plus or minus to each rating.

RESPONSIBILITY	PERFORMANCE RATING	COMMENT (Explanation or Suggestion)
1. **Plans:** Determines what needs to be done by whom by when at what cost for a planning period such as a month, quarter, or year.	G	*needs to share plans with us more.*
2. **Delegates:** Assigns work, responsibility, and authority so his or her people can make maximum use of their abilities.	E–	
3. **Gives Instructions:** Gives day-to-day assignments to his or her people so they do what needs to be done when it should be done in the manner he or she wants it done.	G	*Relies mostly on oral instructions.*
4. **Gets Cooperation:** Helps his or her people work willingly and effectively as individuals and groups.	E–	

RESPONSIBILITY	PERFORMANCE RATING	COMMENT (Explanation or Suggestion)
5. **Solves Problems:** Develops and implements solutions to day-to-day supervisory problems.	G	*Tends to react more than to prevent problems*
6. **Staffs:** Sees that a qualified person is selected for each of his or her positions.	G+	
7. **Trains:** Teaches individuals and groups how to do their jobs.	F	*Little formal training done.*
8. **Motivates:** Determines and helps his or her people meet their personal needs for tangible and intangible compensation over both short and long range.	G+	
9. **Counsels:** Holds a private discussion with an individual about how he or she might do better work, solve a personal problem, or realize ambition.	G−	*See little evidence of counseling.*
10. **Improves:** Develops better methods and procedures to ensure quality and to increase productivity.	G	*No organized improvement effort.*

RESPONSIBILITY	PERFORMANCE RATING	COMMENT (Explanation or Suggestion)
11. **Handles Pressure:** Fulfills responsibility in the face of emotional stress or pressing demands.	*E*	*Stays cool.*
12. **Controls:** Measures progress and takes corrective action when needed to achieve his or her objectives.	*E–*	

OVERALL PERFORMANCE RATING & MOST IMPORTANT
SUGGESTION FOR IMPROVEMENT

G+   Has good people skills but shies away from paperwork. Biggest immediate need is to formalize training so there will be less disruption when new people are added to handle seasonal peak.

If you have a positive experience with the preliminary evaluations you get, you may want additional evaluations from others who can rate your supervisory performance, including your peers. Should your evaluators want anonymity, perhaps you can call on a third party, such as someone in human resources to get and summarize the evaluations.

When you get the evaluations, expect to get reinforcement in certain areas where you perform well. Also be prepared to get a push—an emotional jolt—in those areas where you need to improve. For focus, give priority to only one or two areas of supervisory responsibility. If necessary, get further suggestions from your evaluators about what you need to do. Then take appropriate steps to improve. You may want to get follow-up evaluations a few months later and then perhaps annually.

2. *Solicit informal suggestions for your improvement.* Perhaps you'd rather just talk to people to find out how they rate your su-

pervisory performance and to get their ideas for how you can improve. Your boss, your staff, and your peers are likely to cooperate if you ask them and if they feel you will do something about what they say. One way to find out is to try it.

3. *Conduct an internal customer survey.* You and your people serve others in your organization. They are dependent on your performance and are your internal customers. For example, MIS (management information systems) usually serves all major departments in an organization. Find out how your internal customers rate the performance of the function you head, and you will get an indication of how well you are performing as a supervisor. Their suggestions for improvement will also indicate whether you need to improve your supervisory potential to plan, delegate, give instructions, solve problems, staff, train, or control.

4. *Seek regular guidance from a career sponsor.* For years, I have been acting as career sponsor for a friend of mine. He wants to realize his potential in management, and he gets my counsel every three or four months about how he can meet certain work challenges or continue to develop himself. We have a personal relationship, although he does buy me lunch when we meet. He says my counsel has been helpful and productive.

Do you have or have you ever considered having a career sponsor? If not, think of someone whom you'd like to emulate, and approach him or her. Chances are your intended sponsor has had similar help along the way and would be willing to return the favor. Your sponsor can be someone inside or outside your organization. Do not select someone in the management of your organizational unit, or you will open yourself to accusations of trying to get favored treatment.

5. *Implement a continued program for self-development.* You are more likely to realize your supervisory potential if you accept full responsibility for your own personal development. This means action. You need to develop and maintain a self-development program where you read, take courses and seminars, participate in trade or professional or volunteer organizations, and try to make day-to-day improvements in your supervisory job. If you have a self-development attitude, you will not need much of an emotional jolt to improve. You will try to improve your supervisory performance whenever you see or hear about new or better ways to get planned results through your people.

You can take any or all of the above five actions to find out whether you need to improve your supervisory performance and to give yourself an emotional jolt to improve. But there is another way. And that is to place a summary of *Superior Supervision* where you can see it every day. That summary is shown on pages 5 and 6 in Chapter 1. Periodically, ask yourself if you have fallen into the −10 level of performance. Then ask yourself the extent to which you have +10 performance in each of the twelve areas of supervisory responsibility. Together, the +10 items represent *the 10% solution* for *Superior Supervision*.

As I complete this book, I'm reminded that when one of my sons was in the first grade, he came home with a very good report card. My wife and I complimented him—especially for his "excellent" grade in vocabulary. "What's that?" he asked.

Your people, your boss, your peers, and those you serve provide you with a day-to-day report card. They may not know what *Superior Supervision* is, but you do. And that's all that counts.

Index

About the Author

RAYMOND O. LOEN is a management consultant in Lake Oswego, Oregon. He has over 30 years of management consulting experience plus line and staff management experience with two national firms.

His first supervisory experience was as an officer in the United States Navy. In business, his first supervisory position was city sales manager. Later he became supervisor of a management services group and a supervisor in his own business. In consulting, he has conducted supervisory seminars throughout the country.

He is a founder and board member of Swift Energy Company (NYSE). He has served on the boards of Graphic Software Systems, Lancet Medical Industries, and United Medical Laboratories.

He is the author of *Manage More By Doing Less*, a book published in seven languages by McGraw-Hill, and a 20-hour multimedia program, *Supervising By Objectives*, published by Addison-Wesley. He has written for many business publications including the *Harvard Business Review*.

He has both undergraduate and graduate degrees from the Columbia University School of Business.